MA Creative Writing

Designed for those who are dedicated to their writing and want to see it in print, the renowned MA in Creative Writing at Royal Holloway, University of London is now in its 10th year. Directed and taught by Andrew Motion and Jo Shapcott, with Susanna Jones, Kate Williams, Kristen Kreider and Kei Miller, we offer five groundbreaking pathways in:

• Fiction   • Poetry   • Poetic Practice

Full-time and part-time places are available, all taught at our central London base in Bedford Square, Bloomsbury.

For more information visit:
royalholloway.ac.uk/english    @RHULEnglish

7254 02/15

ROYAL
HOLLOWAY
UNIVERSITY
OF LONDON

Alberto Manguel

Photograph by Melik Külekci

Curiosity

Curiosity has been seen through the ages as the impulse that drives our knowledge forward *and* the temptation that leads us toward dangerous and forbidden waters. In this eclectic history of human curiosity, Alberto Manguel offers a great feast of ideas and a delightful memoir of a reading life. Through examples of famous thinkers who persistently asked 'Why?' he explores how curiosity inspires the imagination to soar.

51 b/w illustrations Hardback £18.99

GRANTA

12 Addison Avenue, London W11 4QR | email editorial@granta.com
To subscribe go to www.granta.com, or call 020 8955 7011 in the United Kingdom,
845-267-3031 (toll-free 866-438-6150) in the United States

ISSUE 131: SPRING 2015

PUBLISHER AND EDITOR	Sigrid Rausing
MANAGING EDITOR	Yuka Igarashi
ONLINE AND POETRY EDITOR	Rachael Allen
DESIGNER	Daniela Silva
EDITORIAL ASSISTANTS	Luke Neima, Francisco Vilhena
MARKETING AND SUBSCRIPTIONS	David Robinson
PUBLICITY	Aidan O'Neill
TO ADVERTISE CONTACT	Kate Rochester, katerochester@granta.com
FINANCE	Morgan Graver
SALES	Iain Chapple, Katie Hayward
IT MANAGER	Mark Williams
PRODUCTION ASSOCIATE	Sarah Wasley
PROOFS	David Atkinson, Amber Dowell, Katherine Fry, Jessica Kelly, Vimbai Shire
CONTRIBUTING EDITORS	Daniel Alarcón, Anne Carson, Mohsin Hamid, Isabel Hilton, A.M. Homes, Janet Malcolm, Adam Nicolson, Edmund White

(your words here)

There's a long history of writing women
(*writers*) off. It's time to right that wrong,
to get relevant not relegated.

Visualizing is for the work. **Galvanizing**
is for getting the work out there. We can
see your words here. So can publishers,
agents + scholars. **Can you?**

Until it's just about the art.
Submit your literary work now.

PEN + BRUSH
www.penandbrush.org

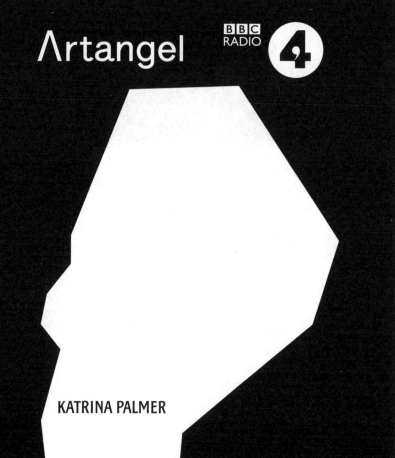

Λrtangel

BBC RADIO 4

KATRINA PALMER

A broadcast on BBC Radio 4
The Quarryman's Daughters

A book consisting of
End Matter

An audio walk on Portland
The Loss Adjusters

May – June 2015
artangel.org.uk/katrinapalmer

Commissioned by Artangel and BBC Radio 4

Supported using public funding by
ARTS COUNCIL
ENGLAND

ARTS COUNCIL
ENGLAND

CONTENTS

Introduction

In the film *Birdman*, there is a note stuck in the frame of a mirror in a seedy dressing room: 'A thing is a thing, not what is said of that thing.' This enigmatic sentence, connected to Raymond Carver's story 'What We Talk About When We Talk About Love' (a play within the film), echoes our title, 'The Map Is Not the Territory'. The phrase was coined by the scholar Alfred Korzybski in the early 1930s to illustrate the distinction between perception and reality. The pieces in this issue of *Granta* are all concerned, in one way or another, with the difference between the world as we see it and the world as it actually is, beyond our faulty memories and tired understanding.

Some of the fiction transcends reality altogether. China Miéville's 'The Buzzard's Egg', a monologue by a guard in charge of a minor captured deity, is one of them:

Good morning.

No? Are you still sulking?

Fine. Be sullen. It makes very little odds to me. I get my food either way.

'The Gentlest Village', an extract from Jesse Ball's *A Cure for Suicide*, is another:

—This is a chair, said the examiner. A person is made in such a way that he can sit where he likes. He can sit on the ground,

she knelt and patted the floor.

— Or even on the table itself,

she patted the table.

These compelling and curiously timeless stories seem to me part of the present zeitgeist. They are not exactly futuristic, but then we live in the future, of course: this world of digital devices, of a creeping loss of privacy, of machine conceptions and unmanned missions to Mars and Comet 67P.

The non-fiction pieces in this issue remind us of the human cost associated with the divergence of map and territory. Janine di Giovanni writes about the sense of doom in Iraq before the American invasion. The map, for the coalition forces, was political abstractions and doctored reports; the territory real life in a real country. The degree of difference between the two correlates to the calamity that ensued.

Arenas of conflict in the world evoke their own media clichés. But the Palestinian writer Raja Shehadeh's gentle memoir about the loss of his mother goes beyond the language of occupation, which makes it all the more powerful. Similarly, Ludmila Ulitskaya's piece, 'Life and Breasts', is about cancer, but it is also a terse commentary on the present state of Russia. Like many people who lived through Communism, which made the distinction between image and reality a political art form, Ulitskaya's writing is stubbornly dedicated to real life in all its surprising details:

> My breast is completely absent: there is even a dent. It has been interred in a special burial ground at the Givat Shaul Cemetery. Lesha Kandel buries all the amputated Jewish appendages from his orthopaedic department there. 'For some reason, Muslims and Christians seem totally unconcerned where their removed organs or body parts lie,' is what he said.
>
> My left breast is at rest in the land of Israel. Perhaps only a first instalment! ∎

Sigrid Rausing

THE GENTLEST VILLAGE

Jesse Ball

I

—This is a chair, said the examiner. A person is made in such a way that he can sit where he likes. He can sit on the ground,

she knelt and patted the floor.

— Or even on the table itself,

she patted the table.

— However, if you are in company, it is best to sit in a chair unless there is a good reason to sit elsewhere. In a chair, one can sit with good posture, that is, with the skeleton set into good order.

He looked at her with puzzlement.

—The skeleton, she said, is a hard substance, hard like wood, like the wood of this chair. It is all through the inside of your body, and mine. It keeps us stiff, and allows our muscles something to pull and push on. That is how we move. Muscles are the way the body obeys the mind.

— Here, she said. Come sit in the chair.

JESSE BALL

She gestured.

The claimant came across the room slowly. He moved to sit in the chair, and then sat in it. He felt very good sitting in the chair. Immediately he understood why the house was full of chairs.

—They put chairs wherever someone might sit.

—They do, she said. And if your needs change, you can move chairs from place to place. Come, let us eat. We shall walk to the kitchen, and there we will get the things we shall eat; also, we will get the things on which we shall eat, and the things with which we shall eat. We will not eat our food there; we'll go to the dining room, or to the enclosed porch. This will be a nice thing for us. Having gotten the food and the implements, we will decide whether we want to eat on the porch or in the dining room. Do you know how we will decide that?

The claimant shook his head.

—You do. Think carefully. Say what comes to mind.

— If it is a nice day, outside . . .

— That is one reason, one of many reasons, why a person would choose to sit outside. It is a good reason. It is always best to have a good reason for doing things, a reason that can be explained to others if you must. One should not live in fear of explaining oneself – but a rational person is capable of explaining, and even sometimes likes to do so.

— Rational?

— A person whose life is lived on the basis of understanding rather than ignorance.

— Am I ignorant?

— Ignorance is not about the amount of knowledge. It is about the mechanism of choosing actions. If one chooses actions based upon that which is known to be true – and tries hard to make that domain grow, the domain of knowledge – then he will be rational. Meanwhile, someone else who has much more knowledge might make decisions without paying any attention to truth. That person is ignorant.

— A mechanism, she continued, is the way a thing is gone about.

They went into the kitchen. On the wall was a painting of a woman feeding chickens with millet. The millet poured from her hand in a gentle arc. Around about her feet the chickens waited in a ring, looking up at her. When the arc made its way to the ground, they would eat.

Beside it was a photograph of a hill. There was a hole somewhere in it.

The claimant paused at these wall hangings, and stood looking. The examiner came and stood by him.

— What is different about these? she asked him.

He thought for a while.

— About them?

— What's the difference between them? I should say. When I say, what is different about these, I am making two groups – them and the rest of the world. When I say between them, I am setting them against each other. Do you see?

— This one happens less often.

JESSE BALL

He pointed to the woman with the chickens.

— Less often?

— If you go looking for them, outside the house, he said, you could probably find the other one, no matter when you looked. But, you can't find this one.

—Why not? Because it is a painting?

— A painting?

— Because it is made by hand – with strokes of a brush? Or for another reason?

— I didn't mean that, he said. I am tired. Can I sit down?

—Yes, let's go to our lunch. We can return to this later.

2

The claimant sat watching her. He was in something she called a window seat. She had her hands folded and was sitting in a chair. They were in a room with what she called a piano. It made loud noise and also soft noise.

The examiner was a girl. The claimant didn't know that word, but it is how he saw her. He had known others, he was sure of it. Her soft yellow hair fell about her shoulders, and her bones were thin and delicate. He felt that he could see where the bones were through the skin. His own bones were larger.

She was helping him. He didn't know why. It occurred to him that he hadn't asked.

—Why am I here? he said suddenly.

The examiner looked up from her book. She smiled.

— I was waiting for you to ask that. Actually, she looked at a little clock that lay across her leg, it is just about the right time for you to be asking that. Nearly to the minute.

She laughed – a small, distinct laugh.

—You are here because you have been very sick. You almost died. But, you realized that you were sick, and you went to get help. You asked for help, and you were brought here. It is my job to make you better. You and I shall become good friends as you grow stronger, and as you learn. There is much for you to learn.

— But, he asked, where was I before?

— In a place like this, she said. Or in some place so different as to be unknowable to us when we are here. I can't say.

—Why do I keep falling asleep?

—You are learning – learning a great deal. It is too much for you, so your body bows out. Then you wake up and you can continue. It will be like this for a time. I have seen it before.

— Are you the only one like me? he asked.

— No, no, no.

She laughed to herself.

—There is a whole world full of people like us. Soon, you will meet others, when you are ready.

— How will we know?

— I will know, she said.

3

On the third day, she pointed out to him a gardener. The man was in the distance, trimming a bush.

—There, she said. There is one.

He stood and watched the man for at least an hour. The man had gone away, and the claimant stood looking at the bush that had been clipped, and at the place where the man had been. He asked the examiner if the gardener was likely to be in that spot again. Not that exact spot, she said, but another near to it. This was the gardener window, then, he said. I can watch the gardener from here. They are all gardener windows, she said. There are others, and others. It's a matter of how far you can look, and if things are in the way. She took him to another window. Out of that one, he could see three people in a field, in the extreme distance. They were scarcely more than dots, but they were moving. At this distance, she said, you can't tell if they are men or women. They could even be children, he said. It might be hard to see a child that far off, she said. They could be, he insisted. The examiner did not tell him: there are no children in the gentlest village.

On the fifth day, she told him about fire, and explained what cooking was. He found fire to be very exciting. He could hardly bear the excitement of it. She wrote this down.

On the sixth day, he closed a cupboard door on his hand, and cried. She explained crying to him. He said that it felt very good. In his opinion, it was almost the same as laughing. She said that many people believe it is the same. She said there was perhaps something to that view, although of course it appeared to be a bit reductive.

4

She wrote things in her notes, things like: Claimant is perhaps twenty-nine years of age, in good health. Straight black hair, grayish-brown eyes, average height, scars on left side from (childhood?) accident, scar under left eye, appears to be a quick learner, inquisitive. Memory is returning relatively quickly. Claimant is matching given data with remembered data – a troubling development.

5

On the morning of the seventh day, he refused to get up. She told him to get up. He refused.

—What's wrong?

—The other day, you said that I almost died. That I was sick and that I almost died.

—You were sick. Now you are convalescing. You are regaining your strength. You are young and have a long life ahead of you in a world full of bright amusements and deep satisfactions, but you have been sick, and you must regain your ability to walk far and parse difficult things.

—What did you mean when you said I almost died?

— It isn't very much. It is a small thing. The world is full of organisms. You are an organism. A tree is an organism. These organisms, they have life, and they are living. They consume things, and grow, or they have no life, and they become the world in which other organisms live and grow. You almost became part of the world in which organisms live, rather than that which lives. It is nothing to be afraid of – just . . .

— But it would be the end? he said. There wouldn't be anymore?

— It would be an end, she said. Do you remember the conversation we had, the second night? About going to sleep?

He nodded.

—What happened?

— I went to sleep, and then in the morning everything was still here.

— Death is like that. Only, you work in the world with a different purpose. The world works upon you.

— How did I die?

—You didn't die. You nearly did.

— How?

—We will talk about this later, when you have more to compare it with. Here, get out of bed. Perhaps it is time for us to go for a walk. Perhaps we should leave the house.

He got up and she helped him dress. They had clothes for him, just his size, in a wardrobe that stood against the wall. They were simple, sturdy clothes: trousers, shirt, jacket, hat. She wore a light jacket also, and a scarf to cover her head. He had never seen her do this. I often cover my head, she said, when I go outside. One doesn't need to, but I like to.

They went into the front hallway, an area that he had not understood very well. It appeared to have no real use. But now when the door was opened he could see very well why there should be this thing: front hallway. He went out the door and down the stairs and stood by her in the street. He could feel the length of his arms and legs, the rise of his neck.

Going outside, he thought – it is so nice! The things that he had seen through the window were much closer. He could see houses opposite and, suddenly, there were people inside of them, and lights on. There was no one in the street, though. He walked with the examiner, arm in arm, and they went up the street a ways.

The houses looked very much the same. He said so.

— Do you know, she asked – do you know which one is ours?

He looked back in fright. The houses were all the same. They were exactly the same. He had no idea which one was theirs. She saw his fright and squeezed his arm. I will take you back to it, don't worry. I know which one is ours.

The street wound past more houses, and they gave way to buildings that she called shops. No one was in these shops, but the windows were full of things that she said might be bought. He did not understand, and did not ask.

On down they went to a little lake. Fine buildings were in a circle around the lake. There was a bridge in the lake to a little island (as she called it), and on the island there was a small house with no walls. They sat in it, and she poured him a glass of water from a pitcher that sat on a tray on a bench at the very center.

6

When he woke up, he was back at the house again, in bed. It was the afternoon, he guessed – as light was all in the sky.

— Did I fall asleep again?

But she was not in the room. He went out to the landing. There was a carpet, but the old wooden boards of the house creaked beneath his feet. He winced, trying to step as quietly as possible. The railing ran along the top of the landing. The balusters were worked with lions and other beasts. He knelt by the edge and listened.

She was speaking to someone else. He couldn't hear what she was saying. The door shut, and she came up the stairs. When she saw him kneeling there, she smiled.

— Did you wake already?

—Who was that?

— Friends. They helped to bring you here. You didn't think I could carry you all by myself?

— Can I see them?

— Not yet, she said.

—What about the other people – the people in the other houses?

— Not yet, she said.

— How will you know?

— I will know.

7

She wrote in her report:

> As I stated before, in the case of this claimant, the dream burden of his treatment was severe. His every sleep period is marred with nightmares. He is still in the first period, prior to Mark 1, so he remembers little to nothing of this, but it is a cause for concern. If it continues this way, I may need to directly address it. He talks in his sleep, muttering about a person who has died, and speaking with a vocabulary that he does not possess during the day. It is my hope that reprocessing is not necessary. He is mid to high functioning and could do very well as things stand but would lose much after a second injection.

She leaned back in her chair and her gaze ran along the wall. There was a stopped clock, an embroidered handkerchief in a glass case and an antique map. The map showed the known world as of a time when nothing was known. How apt for the Process of Villages.

She wrote:

> The previous case that I worked on involved a woman prone to violence and anger. None of that struggle is evident with this current claimant. It appears that his difficulty may have been entirely situational. If that is so, there is a good chance that our process will bring him to balance, as there may be no flaw whatsoever in his psyche.

8

— Gardener is there! He's there!

She came to the window where the claimant was sitting.

— Is it the same one – or a different one?

—This one is wearing . . .

— Glasses.

—The other didn't have them.

— Is that a good way to tell them apart? she asked.

— It is one way.

—What if I were to wear glasses?

She took a pair out of a drawer and put them on.

—Would I be a different person?

She did look like a different person with glasses on, but he didn't want to say that, so he said nothing.

— It is usually safe to assume that a person is different if their physical characteristics are different, said the examiner. But even then sometimes people change – by accident or on purpose – and the same person can look different. Likewise, two people can look very alike.

— Or be exactly the same, he said.

—What do you mean?

—Twins are alike. They are the same.

— But even if the bodies are the same, the minds inside are different – their experiences are different. They are different people.

— Even if they can't be told apart?

— Even then.

— I knew someone, I think, who was a twin.

She looked at him very seriously and said nothing.

— She had a twin, but the twin died.

— How do you know this? asked the examiner.

— I remember it.

— But not from life, she said. You remember it from a dream. When you sleep at night, your mind wreathes images and scenes, sounds, speech, tactile constellations – anything that is sensory – into dreams. One feels that one has lived these things, of course one does. But dreams are imagined. They are a work of the imagination.

— What is the imagination for?

— It is a tool for navigating life's random presentation of phenomena. It enables us to guess.

— But I am sure that I knew her.

— Know her you did, but it was in a dream. You may dream of her again. That is the world where you can meet such a person. The actual world is different. For you, it is this house, and the street beyond. It is the lake at the center of the village, and the gazebo in the lake. It is the meal we take together at midday, and again at nightfall.

She sat for a moment quietly.

— Do you remember the book that I was reading to you from?

— About the poacher and his dog?

— Yes. You remember how real it seemed? Well, it is not real. It just seems to be real. And that is just a toy of words on a page – not anything close to the vibrant power of the mind's complete summoning that you find in the night. Is it any wonder that you believe it to be real? That you confuse memory and sleep's figment?

He shook his head.

She took off the glasses, and put them in the drawer.

— I still feel that you are different with glasses, he said.

She laughed.

— People do look quite different with glasses, I suppose. I suppose that must be true.

—Will you play for me on the piano? he asked.

She went to the piano and opened it.

— I can know that it is you because you play for me on the piano, he said. Someone else wouldn't do that.

— So, she said – you believe an individual's function and service are identical to their person?

She began to play.

He looked out the window again. It was open, and the air was moving now and then, sometimes in, sometimes out. Or, it must move out whenever it moves in. It couldn't just move in, or it would all end up inside. But, he supposed, that wasn't entirely impossible. After all, he was completely inside.

He put his arm out the window and felt the air on it.

Below, the neatly trimmed yard lay flat on its side. The street unrolled from left to right, and beyond the houses, other streets could be seen by the white chalk of their surface. The tops of houses could be seen downhill, the glint of light off the lake in the distance. In the long fields of the distance, and in the canopies of the trees, in waves at their edges, he felt a coy energy. It was as though the edges of things were where the greater part might be hidden – where he could find more.

9

— There is a thing I want to tell you about, she said. It is called naming. Many things have names. You know that. The bottom post on the staircase is called the newel post. The staircase is called a staircase. The post is called a post. The bottom of the staircase is called the bottom. These are all names. People can have names too, and naming is a privilege. In human history, names have been used as a form of power. Poor families, for instance, would sometimes have three or four sons, and those sons would simply be given numbers for names. First son, second son, third son. Some people would be named just for their position. Blacksmith, or Miller. In fact, that naming system was so strong that there remain people today who have as part of their names those old positions.

She paused.

— Can you think of someone you speak about in that way?

— The men who work outdoors.

— You call them gardener. And if you spoke to them that way, they would understand. This is why it is useful – because it is effective communication. You speak to them, and they understand. Now, let us imagine that such a person had a different name – a name that had nothing to do with what he or she did. What would you say to that?

— It wouldn't make sense, he said. How would you get such a name? There would be no reason for you to have it instead of a different name.

—That's true. What would you call me?

— I would call you examiner.

—That's right, and why am I an examiner?

— Because your work is to examine people and things and help to achieve balance.

—That's what I told you, and I have shown it to be true through my actions. So, to you, a sound name for me is examiner. However, that is not my name. That is the name of my position. In the world, there are many examiners, but there is only one person with my particular allotment of cells who stands in my geographical and temporal position. That person is myself, and so I have a name to help differentiate me from other people who are similar to me.

— But, if you are the only one in your circumstance, why do you need a different name? Shouldn't your circumstance alone be the name itself? If it is specific to you?

The examiner laughed.

— Very good, very good. But it isn't necessarily so, because not everyone has perfect information. So, if they saw me on one day at the lake, and then a week later by that distant field, they might not know that I was the same person, unless I had told them my name. If I had, they could speak to me and use my name, and thereby confirm that it was me.

— But what if there were two of you with the same name?

—That is a problem. It is – and it comes up. In any case, I have a name. That gardener has a name. Everyone has a name. Everyone but you.

—Why don't I have a name?

—You don't have a name because you are starting over. You are beginning from the beginning. You are allowed to make mistakes and to fail. You don't need to do that under a real name, a name that will stay with you. We give you the freedom to make every conceivable mistake and have them all be forgotten. So, for now you will have a conditional name. You will have a name while you are here in this first village. Here your name is Anders.

—Anders. Anders.

He said it quietly to himself.

— Can you say it again? Say it again, she said.

—Anders. Anders, he said. But what shall I call you?

—You can call me Teresa. That is not my real name either. It is the name for the examiner that orbits you. Teresa and Anders. Names always function this way, though people don't think about it. They only exist in reference to each other.

—I'm not any more Anders to that gardener than I was a moment ago.

—You aren't. And his name is hidden from you. Perhaps forever.

—Where did my name come from? What does Anders mean?

She thought for a minute.

—I believe it is a Scandinavian name, or perhaps it is German. Let me say completely how it was for me in the moment I named you Anders. That is as close to the meaning of this use of Anders as we can get.

She stood up and went to the window.

—When I was young, there was a girl who lived on the same street as me. Her name was Matilda Colone. She was very pretty and she wore beautiful clothes. She was the envy of everyone at my school, and she was blind. How can that be? Of course, it isn't silly for grown people with circumspection and wisdom to envy a blind person who happens to be extraordinary. However, for children to do so – when the world is so bright and good to look at . . . you may imagine that it is surprising.

He nodded.

— She was elegant and calm. She learned her lessons perfectly. She had a seat in the classroom by a window, and the breeze would ruffle her hair or the scarf she wore, and we would all look at her and look at her and look at her. Matilda Colone, we would say under our breath. The teachers adored her, and everyone wanted to be her friend. But, she needed no friends, and would have none. Of all the things she had, and she had many, the best thing was that she had a brother, named Anders, and he sat beside her in class. He walked beside her to school. He brought her her lunch. He held her coat; he held it up, and then she would put it on. He was very smart, smarter than anyone in the class, except perhaps Matilda, but it was hard to say, because they would never cross each other. It was a school for the smartest children in the region. We all loved her so much that we could almost weep.

—What happened to her?

— This was in the old days. Her father shot himself, and she and Anders were separated and put into homes. Some years after that she died of pneumonia.

— Anders, he said to himself.

IO

Each night, the examiner would say to the claimant something like this (not this, but something like it):

Tomorrow we are going to wake up early. I am going to wake early and you are going to wake early. This will happen because I am sure to do so, and I will come and see to it that you are woken up. Then, I shall dress and you shall dress, and we will go downstairs to the kitchen. In the kitchen, we shall have our breakfast and we will enjoy the morning light. We will talk about the furnishings in the room. We will talk about the paintings and the photographs that we talk about each morning. You will have things to say about them and I will listen. I will have things to say to you about the things you have said. In this way, we shall speak. After breakfast, we will wash the dishes we have used and we will put them away. We will stand for a moment in the kitchen, which we will have cleaned, and we will feel a small rise of pleasure at having set things right. It is an enduring satisfaction for our species to make little systems and tend to them.

Yes, she would continue, we shall go on a walk to the lake, and perhaps this time we will walk around it to the small wood at the back. There we will find the trees that we like. Do you remember them? Do you remember that I like the thin birch that stands by the stream, and that you prefer the huge maple with the roots that block the path? Do you remember when you first saw it, and you ran to it? We shall go there tomorrow, and spend as much time as we want to sitting with those trees, in that quiet place. And when we have done that, we shall come home, walking fast or slow, and we shall . . .

And in this way she would go through the day and give him a sense that there was something to look forward to, and nothing to fear. ∎

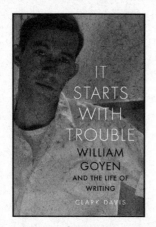

Position Paper

This is my outfit.
Government spooks did the rest. Didn't you know?
Not really. No one is in a hairier place,
my flat mountain.

I'm going to have dinner some night on the ropes.

Bottom line, no one was killed.
That way you retain ownership.
Droopy night brought on by the
old gray mold makers. It was quite . . . unexpected.
That's why I think it's so important
the way squat noses learn, and fast.

Okey doke, I'll tell you in maple shade.
Fast forward to the beginning of your Christmas present.
I have to turn this down,
to clean his pipes,
or clock, whatever.

That's a healing dressing
how many years late—
the continuous way to do it. Sorry. My dizzy.
Pulled pork sliders clogged the glee gate.

No one was killed.

Having a nightgown
under the armpits, darling? Dirt and dare
can be forgiven eyeballing the toiletry lottery
whose torque proclaims it other.

© ANDREY KRASULIN
from *Half*, 2009
Courtesy of the artist

LIFE AND BREASTS

Ludmila Ulitskaya

TRANSLATED FROM THE RUSSIAN BY ARCH TAIT

As we bustle through the joys and trials of life, the unheard drip-drip-drip never stops. Suddenly, though, what we hear is not a melodious tinkling but a stark reminder that life is short, and Death more powerful. Death is here, by our side, and we can make no witty Nabokovian jokes about it.

My reminder of mortality came in early 2010, and I found the narrative that followed raw but completely engrossing. For the present, but only for the present, it is behind me.

When cancer was diagnosed and I found myself facing lengthy treatment, I discovered I was by no means the only one. Several friends had had oncological or other life-threatening diseases before me, others were still ill and yet another received the diagnosis while I was undergoing treatment and was able to offer advice. Vera Millionshchikova and Galya Chalikova will never read this essay, having passed away, taking their own unique insights with them.

There are important things to know. I will list my insights for those who will face the exam in years to come.

A prelude

In the autumn of 2009, the owner of an art gallery came to see my husband. He said, 'Andrey, I'm staging an exhibition. It's going to be called Half.'

'Half of what?' Andrey asked.

'Just the concept. Half of anything.'

Andrey shrugged.

When I arrived later, he told me about it.

'Oh,' I said, 'the bright ideas of these curators are such a pain,' and went back to my half of our apartment. But I thought about the question of how you could physically represent a half. I love solving other people's problems for them, so I went to my chest of drawers, found a pretty French brassiere, took a pair of scissors and cut it in half. I carried it through to the studio.

'How about that, Andrey? A half.'

He put a canvas on a stretcher and pinned the half brassiere to it. I have to say the form was ideal, though it was a pity the bra was so old.

Months passed before the irony of my metaphor could be appreciated.

Anamnesis

I am descended, on my mother's side, from generations of sumptuously endowed women. Although most people have been nourished at a woman's breast, this was especially true in our family. While my grandfather was gainfully occupied in Stalin's prison camps, my grandmother taught herself to sew bras. Her day job was bookkeeping, but her night-time profession was bra-sewing. She was the big-bosomed mainstay of our family, the epitome of human nobility and dignity. Her bovine proportions (not those of some scrawny cow on a Soviet collective farm) and the truly regal bosoms that preceded her were a focus of my flat-chested, prepubescent, intense admiration.

By the time I was twelve I had reached puberty, and it was already clear that I was not to inherit the buxomness of the matrons of my family. Grandmother made my first bra, although there was precious little in need of support.

She viewed my maidenly breasts with surprise and a degree of envy. We small-breasted women know nothing of carrying a burden of many kilograms that can never be set down. We know nothing of the impress of the broad straps of a mammary harness, or the damp patches of irritation beneath a perspiring udder in summertime.

My breasts were an inheritance from my paternal grandmother, a woman who, in her youth, had been an avant-garde dancer and disciple of Isadora Duncan. I did inherit more from her, but relatively little: my hands, my feet, bad handwriting and a vague inclination towards the arts. As a Pisces, I passionately want incompatible things: one part of my nature is attracted to rigorous scientific research, the other to the arts. My first profession was genetics, my second putting pen to paper. The bohemian element emerged the victor, but deep down the scientific side of me feels disdain for it. And, as befits those born in the Tibetan year of the goat, I need good pasture, and will pay almost any price to escape being inconvenienced.

When, in due course, menopause arrived, it brought a major inconvenience: hot flushes. Day and night I was flooded with waves of heat, weakness and sweating. No way was I going to put up with it. An American friend who had been working for over twenty years in a laboratory dealing with fertility problems offered me hormone replacement therapy. Two days after I began taking it, the hot flushes disappeared and I forgot all about them.

I remembered ten years later, and again five years after that, when I tried to stop the treatment. The hot flushes returned instantly, and I resumed taking my favourite pills. The reader will appreciate that as a biologist by training I was fully aware that hormone replacement therapy was rumoured to be dangerous for people with a predisposition to cancer, but I have such an aversion to inconvenience!

And I did have a predisposition to cancer. Nearly all my relatives of the preceding generation had died of cancer: my mother, father, grandmother, great-grandmother and great-grandfather. They had died from different types of cancer and at different ages: my mother at fifty-three, my great-grandfather at ninety-three. I knew the risks. As a civilised person, I went for screenings at the recommended intervals. In our God-given fatherland, women under sixty are given an ultrasound scan, while those over sixty get a mammogram. I attended these screenings conscientiously, despite the casual attitude to health so deeply rooted in Russia: the national fear of doctors, our fatalistic attitude towards life and death, lethargy and a peculiarly Russian sense of irresponsibility. For completeness, I should mention that the Moscow doctors who carried out the screening failed to notice my tumour for a good three years, but that I learned only after the operation.

Biopsy!

In Moscow, I kept trying to go for a check-up, and rang the Ministry of Defence clinic a dozen times. It is within walking distance of where I live, but I couldn't get an appointment. The doctor there was very pleasant, but she was either away on holiday or not on duty. I had been going to her for screenings for several years. It is not a specialist clinic, but I was reluctant to go to the Radiology Institute, of which I had bad memories and which, in any case, was far away. I finally got to see this doctor, who first examined my breasts, then did an ultrasound, then a mammogram, and then pulled a long face. Has it been like this for long? 'Yes,' I said.

I knew, of course, that an inverted nipple was a worrying sign, but when I had come to see her eight months before it had been no different. She had made no comment about it then and neither did I. The tests had shown nothing and I did not want a lot of unnecessary hassle. But now the tests were showing plenty. The doctor wailed, 'Get an urgent appointment with an oncologist! You need a biopsy!'

By now it was March, and I was into a second year of trying to finish a highly recalcitrant novel. How urgent was 'urgent'? I was going to a book fair in Israel in early May, so why not get examined and treated there? I had no wish to return to the Radiology Institute, where my mother had worked for twenty years and where she had died from reticulum cell sarcoma. Neither did I fancy the Blokhin Cancer Research Centre, where two of my friends had died and where they seem to do everything they can to make bad situations worse. I had also heard rumours of bribery and extortion. I do not mind paying at a cash desk, but I refuse to pay under the counter.

I phoned Lika, a friend in Jerusalem. She found a surgeon she said was very good, at Hadassah, the largest hospital in the city. It was sorted, then: I would go there, not tomorrow, of course, but next month, when I would be there anyway for the book fair. I was still living my life in the old way, where plans are adjusted so everything fits in conveniently. I was in denial about who was outside, knocking on my door.

At this point, my friend Lyalya took me in hand. She had a relative who was in charge of immunology at the Blokhin. He would arrange for their oncologists to examine me. It was the end of March and I categorically did not want to go anywhere near the Blokhin Centre but, as an accommodating sort of person, I went anyway.

Lyalya's relative was agreeable enough. He had a luxuriant moustache that reminded me of an animal whose name I could not for the moment remember, and took me to see his friend, a surgeon. This gentleman was quick on the uptake, but cold-blooded. He squeezed my breasts and said he would do a biopsy. Right now. He took a needle practically as thick as a finger and stuck it into me. It hurt, but that was the least of my problems. They examined the slides two hours later and the lab technician gave me a crumpled piece of paper the size of a tram ticket with the word 'Cancer' scrawled on it. A typical Russian detail was that after the word 'Cancer' there were some numbers. I asked what they stood for and was told by the lab technician, who had informed me of her conclusion for a trifling two thousand roubles, that this was a code number for the type of cell. So what cell was that? I asked. She narrowed mulish eyes and declared it a secret she could divulge only to a doctor.

What power she was enjoying! Well, I would be in Israel within a month and a half. I was not going to go berserk and start rushing around seeing doctors. I was scheduled to give a talk in St Petersburg before that, and I did. One night on the train there and one night back.

The new train was amazing. An orthopaedic mattress, a washbasin . . . they all but served dinner in bed! It was as if I was starting life again. I remembered a trip to Pushkin Hills in Pskov Province with a crowd of student friends in the train's corridor, and a hotel in Mikhailovskoye with unspeakable sanitation in the form of a shit-caked drainpipe topped with a commode. How quickly life changes. Everything just gets better and better.

Actually, I now found myself in miraculous surroundings where everybody took great pains to be nice and to look after me: my husband, my children and all my friends! Everybody was offering lifts, looking out for me, eager to protect me. A wonderful circle of friends: I was very happy. How many people loved me! How I loved them! Never in my life had I known such a concentrated outpouring of love. All mine! I had heard I was even being prayed for by those who knew how to do it.

When it was finally time to go to Israel, Marina Livanova got me to Domodedovo Airport with the help of her student Sasha. The things she brought me for the journey! A CD player with CDs, comfortable headphones, sunblock, a little envelope with Florentine notepaper (which could really only be used for writing love letters), a big apple and more besides. A Theatre of Life! How beautifully she does these things. And then she thanked me for giving her so much pleasure. Good heavens!

Vera Millionshchikova, meanwhile, was in intensive care, recovering from a medical overdose, a doctor's error. You do not pay for medical treatment in Russia. You do not pay for behaving irresponsibly. In fact, nobody pays for anything.

From my notebook

Landed in Israel. Lika took me to her doctor at Hadassah Hospital, Dr Zamir. In Hebrew the name refers to a bird which is like a cross between a skylark and a nightingale, only bigger. Actually, he looks more like a Canada goose. Palpates: 'I am not convinced there is cancer.' These doctors' fingers are repositories of sensitivity, a different kind of organ from those of ordinary mortals (which are also wonderful, when not used for killing). Sends me for tests. A young, inexperienced nurse repeats the mammography three times. Then on to another doctor, whose name I do not remember, from South Africa, in a skullcap, with a stubbly white beard. He smells like my great-grandfather: old age, decrepitude, orderliness, old books. More palpating, but no call for a biopsy. Says, 'I can't see anything' (with his hands) 'other than a haematoma.' Also not convinced there is cancer, but sends the optical microscope slides from Moscow to a friend in Haifa who still remembers how to read them – virtually the last doctor in Israel familiar with this antediluvian methodology. I was taught to make histological sections for glass slides at the Institute of Paediatrics forty years ago. Nobody does it nowadays.

Surprise at the diagnosis 'Cancer', a term no longer used here. Cancer cells now have a first and last name (concealed, in Russia, behind those secret numbers). A strange feeling that all this must unquestionably be happening. I pretend everything is only what I was expecting all along. At the same time I seem to be watching from the sidelines, observing what this elderly Russian woman is saying and how she is behaving. She completely refuses to act her age, feels fine, feels lucky, sees herself surrounded by a crowd of close, much-loved family, friends and admirers. It is not self-possession: cancer is like a flavour enhancer in cooking, showing me how wonderful life around me is.

I am looking from a distance at an amazing picture composed of the beauty of this wonderful spring: Jerusalem, my doctors and my amazing friends. Who needs a Wailing Wall? The diagnosis has not been quashed, but suspended. My cancer does not hurt. I will die soon anyway, but not tomorrow. I see as never before what Yevgeny Popov dubbed the 'beautifulness of life'. What an expression!

Another undeservedly beautiful day. Sasha Okun drives me to Haifa, telling me about his trip to Munich. He saw an exhibition of Rubens who, out of sheer boredom, made copies of the paintings in the Escorial when he was in Spain. We talk about all sorts of things on the way. A delight. I am really interested because I have not read much and Sasha knows more about art than anyone else, from the inside, intimately. He is a major artist himself, but not like Andrey. A different lineage. He has some affinity with Lucian Freud, but combined with a great sense of humour and vitality. Profoundly versed in philosophy and literature.

Rambam Hospital in Haifa. The doctor a ginger-and-grey-haired Russian speaker. About forty-five and a top man. A pleasure just to watch him focusing the microscope. He confirms cancer, a carcinoma, in the Moscow slides. At last I know! Two punctures, quite painful, but nothing found on the new slides. The haematoma still not resorbed.

Back to Jerusalem, and preparations get under way: computer tomography very unpleasant, involving two litres of some revolting liquid and then having dye injected into a vein. Main thing is for them not to find any metastases. Meanwhile, the opening of the book fair, with interviews, meetings, rushing about. I am so tired, ready to drop. Things are moving quickly: a new biopsy shows a carcinoma fairly resistant to chemotherapy and seemingly more aggressive than adenocarcinoma. Breast cancer, labile, ductal, making diagnosis difficult.

The imaging is not ready, and I expect more bad news when it is. Everything has become more serious. The surgeon sends me back to the oncologist in Ein Karem. I am working in all my spare time. The Lord seems to have heard my remark that I dread longevity. Be that as it may, I have a novel to finish.

Last days of April. My dreams are very powerful. There are grimy chalices with dull glass in them. Cleaned up, it turns out to be jewellery: pendants, earrings, diamond and coloured red, green and blue. An elderly woman comes and says, 'Those are mine!' 'No problem,' I say, handing them over without regret.

In another dream there is a strange, rounded metal object of uncertain purpose, half the size of a fist and pleasant to touch. I hold it in my hand, showing it off.

2 May. After the oncologist, the fair. I fit everything in, get everywhere on time. Tomorrow, a preoperative consultation.

A talk: the left breast is to be removed. What happens after that we have to wait and see. If the express analysis reveals cancer cells in the lymph glands, all the nodes will be removed. If not, we can avoid chemotherapy.

The cells are hormone-dependent, so if there is chemotherapy, it will be a new, targeted variety, blocking receptors. The patient must be kept informed. I like knowing.

The plan is to operate, then take a break. After two or three weeks of recovery, chemotherapy, depending on what is found. It probably will be needed.

Dr Zamir says he finds my sangfroid disquieting. He has not seen it before. Normally the women who sit in this chair cry. Then, by taxi to Mishkenot Sha'ananim (Refuge of the Carefree: I am right

LUDMILA ULITSKAYA

at home here). Memorise that word. Do not forget it! The centre is near the nineteenth-century Montefiore Windmill. All the writers at the book fair are put up here.

At 9 p.m. I go to bed, this time in a hotel room. I will get up early and look out from the gallery over the Old City. I may even go for a walk. At two in the afternoon I have to be at the hospital for nuclear magnetic resonance imaging. At seven thirty a meeting with the writer Meir Shalev. A packed programme: half book fair and half medical tests.

6 *May*. A round table with three authors. 'Humour and death'. Ironic, given the circumstances. Andrey Kurkov, Michail Grobman and me. Grobman highly illogical. Introduced as a representative and theorist of a second avant-garde movement. Starts off with a lot of nonsense about how the new kills the old. Naive, old-fashioned drivel. Next he reads his monstrously racist anti-Arab poem. It is a disgrace. In case that is not enough, he adds that anyone who still says they like Bulgakov is an idiot. We clash primly. He insists on the primacy of ideology in literature, on a new, higher level, so to speak. We've been there and done that already.

All my free time I spend in *The Big Green Tent*. For the first time, the title came to me before the novel. All sorts of things are happening in it now. Liza reappears at the peak of her career. She has a duet with Richter, a tour, competitions. The misery of the Brezhnev era. We are in a place not even music can reach. The death of Mikha, deep depression. Liza marries a conductor, a German, a Bavarian probably. Pierre sends a messenger, his American fiancée, after Sanya. She sobs on his shoulder: 'I do not need a fur coat, I do not need money.' Based on the saga of Gennady Shmakov.

I almost forgot a trip with Okun to the Monastery of St John in the Desert. A touching icon of Elizabeth with him as a child. A very old, very poor little Greek church made of bricks. We see no monks, but visit the cave of St John and the springs, the kind of place where you have no doubt something did happen. No sense of emptiness.

On the way back, we eat at an Indian cafe. It was closed but they give us the leftovers from a tourist group they had catered for. Two mothers with babies. While they are making coffee for us, I hold one of the babies, which is quite lovely.

Okun is in and out of hospital now with lung trouble. For his wife it is her bladder. Sasha's mother is ninety-six, also a kind of terminal diagnosis. Everybody is ill, not just me. But Vera Millionshchikova is feeling better.

8 May. I almost slept through last night. Hot flushes receding. My left breast will be removed soon. An uneasy feeling of something disagreeable going on in my armpit. It is worrying. Sensations in my left breast and left armpit. Feels like something growing. Not too much, I hope, in the three days remaining before the surgery. After that I will learn to live without a left breast, at the very least. And who knows for how much longer. I am anxious to finish that book.

They continue palpating my armpits. ECG, another blood test. Everything depends now on the express analysis. I am in a very good mood. Tomorrow they will put a marker in my breast, for the surgeon. I am battling with *Tent.*

An X-ray, not diagnostic but to indicate the position of the glands for the benefit of the surgeon, expertly done by an Arab doctor or male nurse. I sit in the university park, among bushes and flowers, on a secluded bench where it is shady and cool, waiting. The temperature is thirty-eight degrees but you do not feel it here. Today is Jerusalem Day, the anniversary of the liberation of the city in 1967. The Arabs are not celebrating much, understandably.

13 May. Today my left breast was removed. Technically, it was brilliant: no pain at all. This evening I am lying in bed, reading, listening to music. Incredible anaesthetic plus two spinal injections in the roots of the nerves leading to the breast. No pain. To my left is a bag for vacuum-suction drainage. 75 ml of blood. To my right a cannula for transfusion. Antibiotics as a precaution.

Lika with me all day. She came at seven in the morning and sat with me until eight in the evening. She is an angel. Lyuba peeped in. An unimaginable comfort in these circumstances. Most importantly, analysis found no carcinoma in the lymph nodes. My armpit is left alone. In a week's time a histological check before deciding how to proceed.

My neighbour in the ward is a kindergarten teacher from the north, on a pension. She was supposed to have her operation in Haifa but wanted Dr Zamir. Theoretically she should have to pay 18,000 shekels, but insurance covers 15,000, leaving her just three thousand to pay – less than one thousand dollars. In effect, everything is free. This is socialised medicine. My neighbour too had that very latest injection and is not in pain.

I am here privately, but special. Dr Lesha Kandel is a friend, and Vladimir Brodsky, the chief anaesthesiologist, is a friend of his. All the Russian doctors are coming to me for book signing. VIP! Aside from the interest in my books, everybody else gets exactly the same treatment, only without paying.

Poor Russia! 145 million people going under the knife without anaesthetic, rolled in the dirt and infected in hospitals with God knows what. Poor Alla Belyakova. They found she had bowel cancer. The Blokhin Centre said, 'Go away, it's too late!' She was admitted in Troitsk, south of the Urals, and is delighted. It is a horrible cancer, and poor Andrey, her son, is autistic. What will become of him?

My breast is completely absent: there is even a dent. It has been interred in a special burial ground at the Givat Shaul Cemetery. Lesha Kandel buries all the amputated Jewish appendages from his orthopaedic department there. 'For some reason, Muslims and Christians seem totally unconcerned where their removed organs or body parts lie,' is what he said.

My left breast is at rest in the land of Israel. Perhaps only a first instalment!

I am staying with Lika. A strong draught blows through the apartment. Something slithers, and then falls, in the kitchen. I go in and close the window. On the floor is a picture that had been on the fridge. It is by an Israeli artist, Miriam Gamburd, exhibited in Paris in 2001. Fleshy, busty women are taunting an Amazon who is central to the composition. She has her hand on one breast. The other, the left breast, has been amputated. We are stunned. The picture had been there for ages but we only noticed it today.

So many mysterious, significant happenings. My world is protecting me: my friends, friends of friends, their relatives, the doctors. Everyone is looking after me, and pride of place goes to Lika.

In spite of everything, it has come together wonderfully. There is so much joy here. I should have a small ex-voto silver breast made and hang it in church on an icon of St Panteleimon or someone, even if the breast was not actually saved. Good Lord, it has been done already – Andrey's 'half' was my ex-voto!

Poor breast! It took me such a long time to get round to saying goodbye. Of course, it had behaved very badly, but I have a lot more to apologise for. Seventeen years of hormone replacement therapy!

Why am I writing all this? Because I need to develop a new relationship with my body, and primarily with my breasts. As I approach three score years and ten, I have all sorts of things to feel guilty about, but right now I feel worst about what I have done to my poor body. How odd, that after a lifetime of being offhand, even cruel, with my blameless body, I have only realised it now!

This whole story is beyond belief. It looks as if I am going to get away with it, but even if I do not, so much here has been wonderful.

I heard yesterday that Galya Chalikova has stage 4 ovarian cancer with metastases, and ten litres of fluid in her abdomen. I phoned and asked her to consider the Hadassah. The third catastrophe in the last few months: Alla Belyakova, Vera Millionshchikova and now Galya. My own gnat bite hardly merits mention. It is all just heartbreaking.

I am reading *Conversations with Alfred Schnittke*. Brilliant, in places astounding: 'After my stroke there is a lot I do not understand, but I know more now.' Intuitive knowledge. I can allow myself to cry over that. Jerusalem is a city with plenty of places where you can go to weep, but it is not obligatory.

Ten days later. I hear I will need a second operation because a cancer cell has been found in one of the five glands, where the analysis had shown nothing. It is scheduled for 3 June. It will take slightly less time, but the basics are the same: general anaesthetic, drainage, healing. It may hurt more. Afterwards the likelihoods are: five years of hormone treatment, for sure; local irradiation, possibly; and, the worst option, eight courses of chemotherapy at intervals of two weeks, over four months. I am obsessive about making contingency plans, but it seems even the worst option means everything will be done by October. There are, however, more dire possibilities. I am at stage 3 by the Russian definition, but with metastases in the axilla.

It is Trinity Sunday and tomorrow is Monday of the Holy Spirit. It is four in the morning and the megaphone-voice of the muezzin broadcasts the call to prayer. I willingly join him.

I am waiting for it to be morning, and hoping to see Zamir today so I can fit in a lightning trip to Moscow before chemotherapy.

I am writing away at the novel but it shows no sign of coming to a conclusion. I am on edge and tired, I feel unwell, but very happy. In fact, full to overflowing. I discover Gidon Kremer and two other musicians on YouTube clowning about with themes from classical music. Like Nabokov writing about Chernyshevsky, the priest's son playing quite unselfconsciously with his father's censer. Young people amuse themselves by playing with things that are sacred. They are in their element.

A week in Moscow. Hard going. Lots of people, things to do, none of it really necessary. I visit Vera Millionshchikova. She is in remission. Her skin is peeling, her nails growing back, new hair appearing. She is settled in a hospice, on the understanding that she will die.

Jerusalem. I fly back with one day to spare. What do I feel? Nothing. Tomorrow, 3 June, I have the second operation.

The operation was yesterday. I feel all right. My arm is not painful if I do not move it, but is if I make sudden or sideways movements. I will be discharged tomorrow. It is hot, the light is strong and I have an extraordinary sense of clarity, although quite what is clear I cannot express.

Ein Karem

I have been living for over three months in Ein Karem now, and it is one of the most magical places on earth. Until 1948 this was an Arab village, and it became Jewish overnight, as it had been two thousand years ago, when the Arabs left for Jordan on the day Israel declared independence. John the Baptist was born here, and this is where the two most famous Jewish women met, Mariam the mother of Jesus and Elisheba the mother of Johanaan. Mary and Elizabeth. There is a spring where they are said to have met, and a nearby well, where they are also said to have met. You are shown a cave which supposedly housed the dwelling where John the Baptist was born.

Everything here proliferates. Several places claim to be where the mothers met, and there is more than one monastery: St John in the Mountains, the Sisters of Zion, the Sisters of the Rosary and the Russian Orthodox Gorny Convent. From my favourite, the Sisters of Zion Convent, you have the best view towards Jerusalem. I was there yesterday, on the Feast of the Transfiguration of Our Lord. There was no service, because the Orthodox and Catholic calendars are different, and it was too difficult to go up the hill to Gorny. Yesterday the temperature was a record forty-three degrees.

I went into the empty chapel, and then out into the orchard. The fruit is not consecrated, but the trees looked beautiful and seemed none the worse for it. Nearly all the lemons were green. A pear tree had fruit scattered over it like light bulbs. There were a lot of pomegranate trees, the loveliest of all. Most of the pomegranates had a crimson-lilac hue, although some were still green. Others were no longer green but had yet to turn purple. They gleamed like gold in the sun.

Alphonse Ratisbonne, a baptised Jew from France, founded the convent 150 years ago.

The village is in a valley, with the vast Hadassah Hospital above it. Apart from my left breast buried in Givat Shaul, the rest of me is alive, feeling very well, and looking forward to continuing for some time yet to explore the world, to rejoice and reflect on the magical and interesting way that life is arranged.

I have time now to think about what has happened to me. I am undergoing chemotherapy, with radiotherapy to follow. The doctors are optimistic and have decided I have a good chance of coming out of this alive, but of course I know that, ultimately, nobody gets out alive. A strikingly clear and simple thought has occurred to me: illness is a matter of life, not of death. What matters is how we comport ourselves as we walk away from the last home we live in.

There is also the major topic of suffering, which I am thinking about all the time but so far without reaching a conclusion. My ideas would not go down well with any Orthodox priest. It seems to me that suffering simply should not exist. The fact that it can evoke heroic endurance and courage is beside the point.

I am renting a small, single-room Arab house built on the roof of another house, large and incredibly beautiful, one of the most beautiful houses I have ever seen. How the Arabs who had to leave all this behind, almost without warning, must grieve for it still.

Israel inclines you to reflect. The story of this land is all about insoluble problems. It is a minefield of peoples and ideas, a minefield of history. Dozens of tribes have been exterminated, hundreds of languages and ancient communities have been lost. It is a cradle of love, and a place where people choose death. It is the land of revelation (as I do not doubt), but revelations occur in other places too, anywhere. History begins at any point in time.

The Big Green Tent is still not done. I cannot remember a time when

I was just writing it – I seem always to have been trying to finish it.

After my third bout of chemotherapy I could work no longer. I could neither read nor sleep. It was extremely hot in Israel, but in Moscow and the rest of Russia the heat was even more unbearable. My son Petya and his family stayed in Moscow, unable to leave because there were no tickets, or because they had no strength, or because they had nowhere else to go. With two small children at home, they barely went outside the apartment. They installed an air conditioner. The smog was so dense they could not see the next apartment block. It was very distressing. I would have liked them to come to Israel, but they had no passports for foreign travel.

There were three-week intervals between the injections. I was all for flying back to Moscow to see to the children, but everybody advised against it, so I spent another month and a half in Ein Karem. During the worst weeks I hardly came down from my roof. Friends visited me, bringing food I could not bear to look at. Everything lost its taste – eating was like chewing cotton wool.

A miracle occurred. For the past few months I had been listening a lot to music, partly as a professional obligation. The protagonist of my novel is a musician, and I needed to live through this aspect of his inner life. I read a lot of books on music, but by now the drugs had so flattened me that I could only lie there like a dead fish, incapable of doing anything other than listen to it. I began doing so, almost twenty-four hours a day.

I always knew my limits, having given up music school at the age of ten. For many years that joyful sense of liberation defined my relationship with the piano. It was an instrument for torturing children and I avoided it. My happiest memory from those years is the wonderful musical discord I heard walking down the school corridor. Music emanated from every door, merging into a marvellous noise of everything playing at once, new every time.

Ten years passed before I listened to music again. Not Beethoven and Schubert, but Scriabin and Stravinsky, Prokofiev and Shostakovich. I went to concerts at the Scriabin Museum and listened to Mahler. It was great, and very much the in thing, but music was only one cultural component of my life and there was much else besides. Nevertheless, I always knew I was skirting the edge of a dense forest, not venturing into the depths.

Here, in Ein Karem, something happened. New possibilities of perception opened up. Perhaps one side effect of the poisonous chemicals permeating me was to break down a membrane preventing music getting through to me. It was a dramatic change. In the night, up there on my baking hot roof, I listened and listened. Sasha Okun kept me supplied with excellent CDs and I could not have wished for a better guide through the forest. Lika brought a player, which sounded wonderful in Israel but when I moved back to Moscow, it seemed fairly indifferent. Were my ears sealed again?

Seemingly not. I do not know how many times I listened to the Art of Fugue played by Samuel Feinberg, better than Richter in my estimation. Just as many times I listened to the sonatas of Beethoven, Schubert and Haydn, and to so much else. Music was flushing the poison out of my system.

I had more radiotherapy, and in those weeks, bald, weak but in good heart, I again set about finishing my novel.

Hadassah

I moved to another apartment, still in Ein Karem. Now I have a separate house next to the Greek church. On the other side of my fence is the cottage of the caretaker and the priest, apparently the same person. The windows of the church are wide open and I can follow the service from my balcony. My landlord is a devout Jew born in İzmir in Turkey. His wife is from Australia and works at the Hadassah Hospital as a nanny for very small children, of which she has plenty of her own. They are loving parents, not strict, but the children are respectful and cheerful and do as they are told. They invited me one time to Shabbat, a busy table with teenaged sons, daughters and their young friends, a single lady who was a neighbour and me, the tenant. Our host is Sephardic so there was none of that nostalgia for the herring, potatoes and pickled cucumbers of East European Jews. It was Middle Eastern fare, bread and wine – an unfamiliar style, quite different, but with the same prayers and blessings.

Five times a week I went to the hospital, as if I worked there, to be irradiated by the electron gun. An uphill path took me from the village to the hospital and the oncology department. A helicopter pad on the roof can be seen from afar. In wartime the wounded are brought here, delivered within two hours from any part of the country. Israel is small and wars and terrorist attacks are frequent. The hospital is enormous, with as many storeys underground as above. The bottom floor is a locked surgical department, fully operational in case of war. This country respects and takes good care of its soldiers. That is another topic, and any comparison of the lot of Russian and Israeli service personnel can only bring tears and recrimination. We have a lot to learn from the Israelis about how to organise our health services, as well as about the relationship between the army, the government and society.

But I digress. I now have a detailed knowledge of Hadassah Hospital. I know its doctors and nurses, its long passages and corridors covered in plaques with the names of benefactors. 'This chair, piece of equipment, office, department was donated by so-and-so' in memory of a deceased grandmother, grandfather, mother, sister. On the ground floor is a synagogue with stained glass by Marc Chagall, donated by the artist.

This is a state hospital, the largest in the land, and it attracts huge donations from Jews in Israel and all over the world. The traditional tenth of your income paid as a tithe is now most often donated not to a temple but to charity. Scientific research benefits particularly.

The hospital is full of volunteers. Jewish women in wigs push trolleys with drinks and pretzels, or take wheelchair-bound patients for a walk. All citizens of Israel are treated here, Jews and Arabs alike, and the doctors too are both Jewish (half of them from Russia) and Arab. After my surgery I witnessed a comical scene: two patriarchs were wheeled down the corridor towards each other. One was Jewish, wearing a black velvet kippah and Hasidic robe, followed by his wife in a wig and a posse of children, from teenage to very small; the other was a handsome sheikh, resplendent in white cap and robes, with his wife behind him in a richly embroidered dress, and also with a whole brood of children. Both had had surgery for cancer. They drew level, nodded to each other without making eye contact and moved on. Hadassah is a zone if not of peace then of truce. It is like a watering hole: when it is a matter of life and death, passions subside, ideology takes a break and territorial disputes become meaningless. A person needs very little space in a cemetery.

At the hospital, doctors fight for people's lives, and the value of every life is the same. The patient should not suffer pain: that is a principle of all civilised medicine. Ten times a day, during every procedure, you are asked, 'Does that hurt?' One time I replied without thinking, 'It's fine. I can put up with it.' 'What? You are in pain? But that is bad for you! We must stop the pain immediately.'

This is what they are taught at medical school: pain must be prevented. Mine has been the Soviet experience: dentists only recently began anaesthetising their patients. Throughout my childhood and youth they drilled teeth, tore them out by the roots, changed dressings and removed stitches regardless of pain. Unfortunately, I know only too well how difficult it is to get painkillers in Moscow, even for patients in the terminal stages of cancer. Imagine the situation in the provinces. And then there are the maternity hospitals where staphylococcus is endemic. They cannot be sterilised with ultraviolet light from quartz lamps because nothing is capable of sterilising ruins.

These thoughts usually come to me on the way back from radiotherapy. Of course, you do sometimes suffer radiation burns here too, but they protect you as much as possible. A lead shield is moulded specifically for each patient in accordance with their anatomy, to prevent the radiation from damaging the heart and lungs.

Cancer is a cruel disease and, despite the doctors' best efforts, patients are by no means always cured. People die even in the best clinics of America, Germany and Israel. But the situation is far worse in Russia.

I really cannot imagine what it would take to raise our Blokhin Centre to the level of Hadassah.

I walk back down the path, past the accommodation for the medical staff, past the car park, and every rock is familiar, every tree. The wall of the Franciscan monastery is to my right. I go on past, down to the spring where the road divides, up to the Gorny Convent or down to the bus station, with the kindergarten on the left. Here is the turning to the Museum of Biblical History, invariably closed, and then I am back at my house. One wall is built of ancient stones, another of plasterboard, a third of brick. It has been thrown together like the house of Cobbler Pumpkin. The windows are different sizes and the door does not lock. It is getting hotter by the day. I still have not finished my novel. But there is only a little more to write. ■

Courtesy of the author

DREAMED IN STONE

Jon Fosse

TRANSLATED FROM THE NORWEGIAN BY DAMION SEARLS

I

No one saw the avalanche because it all fell apart so slowly. Not day by day, not even hour by hour, or minute by minute, but it fell apart. It was falling apart the whole time, and it was an avalanche. It had to be an avalanche, because what else could it be?

But did it slide like mud?

No, it didn't slide like mud, it was more like a sudden imperceptible jolt.

But someone must have seen it?

No, no one. Or maybe someone did but they didn't want to. Or maybe no one saw it. The jolts were too quick, jolt after jolt.

But in that case you can't really call it an avalanche?

Yes, it was an avalanche, it was an avalanche.

Was there a flaw in the middle somewhere?

Why do you ask that?

I think it happened because there was a flaw somewhere that finally made it come apart.

Maybe, but I think there were lots of smaller cracks, not a big one, lots of almost invisible cracks.

Yes, it could have been like that. But these small almost invisible cracks somehow combined into a big crack, a chasm almost.

There is something almost like joy in your voice.

A chasm.

Yes, yes, like a chasm.

II

I can't stop thinking about how it fell apart so slowly, so imperceptibly slowly.

Yes, you've already said that.

Yes.

But the avalanche itself, it really came so suddenly.

Yes.

Yes. And you're saying there were several avalanches and then it just lay there.

I just lay there.

You just lay there.

Yes I just lay there, on the front steps of my house.

And then?

And then someone said something and I tried to get up, but I couldn't, and someone helped me get up. I stood there. Then I opened a door. I went in and shut the door behind me.

And then?

I don't remember anything. I remember that I woke up and I was lying on the floor inside. I got up. I was standing. I walked.

And then?

I thought I had to go and lie down.

Yes.

Yes. And then I woke up again. I was lying next to the kitchen table. And then I thought I had to go and lie down. I got up. I was standing. I found the sofa and lay down.

III

Three times it fell apart. Everything became black; a kind of fog in my sleep, but with a kind of quivering somewhere inside, like particles of stone in motion, or small stones in a slow avalanche, so slow that it can't be called an avalanche.

Yes, you said that.

Yes.

And then?

No one saw the avalanche.

You were alone.

Yes, I was, yes.

And that's probably why it wasn't an avalanche.

No, maybe not.

But something like that.

Yes.

And then we are quiet for a while.

And now.

Now.

What do you think? About the avalanche. Where did the stones go?

They just lay there, but then they fell apart again.

Yes.

IV

Shards of stone, these stones too, small stones, shining in the grey fog. They shone weakly but they shone, and then the light gathered and I saw that I was lying on a sofa. I stood up. I went out a door. I shut a door behind me. I walked. I stood waiting for a bus. It was hard to stand. And then it fell apart again. I was lying on a sidewalk. I suddenly knew I was lying on a sidewalk. Somebody came running. He helped me up. I was standing. I tried to get on a bus but another man came running and said that I couldn't go by bus, this was not a bus for someone like me, the man said. I asked if I couldn't just sit down on the bus, but no, no, this wasn't a bus for someone like me, he said. I asked the driver, it was a woman, and she smiled and shook her head. She said nothing, or maybe she said no. And then, I think it happened like this if I'm not misremembering, the man who had helped me to my feet came and took me to a car, a taxi. He put me in the taxi and I sat down and the driver and I drove off. The man driving said that he often thought about nothing, how nothingness is in everything. Nothingness is in everything, the taxi driver said.

Yes.

I didn't say anything to him about the stones.

No, of course not.

Nothing about the avalanche.

No, of course you didn't.

And then we were sitting there and neither of us said anything. We sat like that for a long time.

I don't like you talking about the stones and the avalanche. It's fake, in a way, like you're lying.

Yes. It almost feels like that.

But why are you doing it then?

I don't entirely know.

No, it's probably not so easy to know.

V

The stones sing and they don't sing. Even when the fog is gone the stones lie there, leaning against each other, they lie there so nicely, as though they have been put together by a wonderfully dexterous stonemason, they lay there like that after the avalanche too. Falling apart.

Yes, yes.

And then we laugh, yes, we laugh. After the avalanche too.

So then you were sitting in a car. And the man driving said that there was some nothingness in everything, and then what?

It was in a taxi, and we were talking about nothing and about what is behind and in everything that is, it was where it came from, it's there, the man driving said.

The taxi driver.

Yes, him, yes, he said that there is nothing that is God before the beginning, it begins with the Word, he said. Yes, him, the man driving the car, he said that.

That was well said.

It was as if nothing was falling apart. But everything was so grey, like in a fog.

Like grey stone, you said.

Yes. But it was a little lighter in the car.

In the taxi.

Yes.

And then?

Well, then I got out of the taxi and went into the airport. And then it fell apart again. I was lying on the floor and when I looked up there were lots of people around me and someone was taking my pulse and said, he's weak, and then a man with a wheelchair came and put me in the chair and pushed me to a room and I sat there and he said that I might be able to board the plane, they would evaluate me, he said, and he gave me water and then he pushed me in the wheelchair to the plane, ahead of all the other passengers, and when we reached the aeroplane door someone came to meet me . . .

Who?

. . . a flight attendant met me and said, he's allowed on, and then they pushed me into the plane and put me in the front row and someone else . . .

Another flight attendant?

. . . asked if I wanted anything and I said maybe I'd like a little water. And then I was given a little water. Stone and water. Stone, stone and water. And I was an avalanche, shards of stone, and all the stones were in a grey fog that seemed to shine a little from the crushed stones, and they were in perfect order, lying against each other as though they had arranged themselves in a kind of wall. A fine wall.

Yes, you said that already. I am thinking that this talk about the stone and the avalanche is nothing but a lie and concealment, but there might be something in it nonetheless, I think.

A fine new wall.

And then?

And then I was pushed out of the plane in a wheelchair. I said I could walk but I wasn't allowed to because I might fall again, that was why it was best if I was in a wheelchair and then I was taken, yes, you remember that, don't you?

No, it wasn't me who took you.

No, no it wasn't you, it was someone else who took me, and he put me in his car and drove me to my flat. He took me inside, and I lay down, and I lay there and I was an avalanche, I was stone that had become many stones, an avalanche, an avalanche that kept going and I just lay there, and then the avalanche started to move and turn in on itself, I shook, I shook and shook and then shook a little less. I shook and everything was grey stones in the fog and everything was a slow avalanche, slow, and the grey had some white in it, it's not visible as white but is it white is it?

Is it white as snow?

No, it isn't like snow, and it isn't white, but it's like white, it is snow, it's not snow . . . no, it's not white, it's not snow, it is grey, just grey, it is greyer . . . just a simple grey if it weren't for the stones that were still there, the avalanche that had arranged itself so nicely, the stones that lay there so beautifully and quietly even though I shook and shook . . . and my son made dinner for me but I couldn't eat, and he bought me a bottle of vodka and I shook less and was calm and then I slept well there on, or in, those grey shining stones. I slept, I don't remember much more, I remember less and less and then they came with a stretcher and said that I have to get dressed and then you said, he can't manage it, can't you see, and I shook and shook and they agreed that I could put on a bathrobe, that was easy, and then I was lying on the stretcher. And I shook and shook. And I saw that the avalanche was gone. I was the avalanche.

But the stones lay there, in a wall, even if they were falling apart.

I think so. Because it felt like the stones in the avalanche were me.

VI

You were a chasm that cracked and turned into stones, and then the stones lay there, beautifully laid, in a wall.

Yes. Yes that's how it seems to be, it seems like that now.

Yes. And the chasm is gone?

The chasm does not exist any more.

And the stones shine in their own new pattern.

Yes. What used to be a chasm is now between the stones.

The stones laid together make an open room?

Yes.

Is there something in the room?

I think so. I can see something there.

And then we sit in silence.

The man who was saying that nothingness is in everything.

Yes. What about him?

No, nothing.

VII

These slow movements, falling apart, and then the sudden ones, incredibly quick, like sudden gusts of wind. Then the quiet. The big crack with its light, then the slow imperceptible avalanche, and then this sudden movement, this sudden falling apart. And then the stones, grey like fog, but still shining with a faint light instead of nothing, a little light, so weak, almost like ashes, almost like glowing ashes on stone. And then stone on stone. I am in the room behind the wall of stones, my stones, other people's stones, and there is light in there, the strong invisible light from the sky, from the stones. The light of nothingness. The light of nothingness is in the stone. The light of love is in the stone.

VIII

I go in, in behind the stones, and I sit down. I sit and look at the stones. I see that it's me. I am the stones: it's not like me, but like what is I in me. I go out between the stones and take my place, I stand there with outstretched hands, like a cross. I see a cross. I look down. I look up. I sit down. I look at the stones, so beautifully laid, stone on stone, in a wall. I get up. I stand.

IX

And then you hold my hand. And the stones say that love exists, love is.

Weren't you scared?

No, never.

But you almost died.

I wasn't afraid to die.

I am not afraid to die either.

No. ■

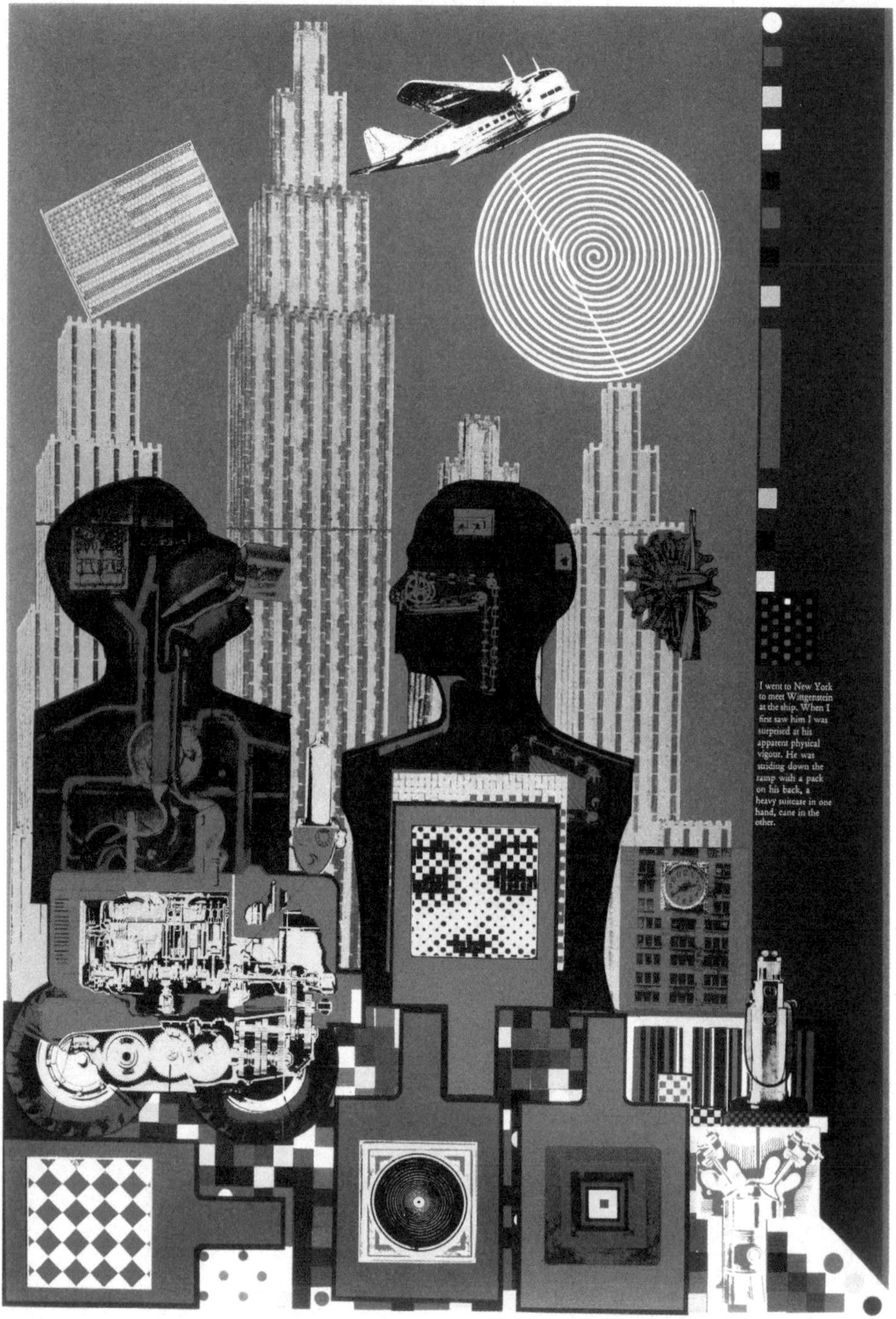
I went to New York to meet Wittgenstein at the ship. When I first saw him I was surprised at his apparent physical vigour. He was striding down the ramp with a pack on his back, a heavy suitcase in one hand, cane in the other.

EDUARDO PAOLOZZI
Wittgenstein in New York, 1964

HER LOUSY SHOES

Tracy O'Neill

He thought about what he'd say to Miranda if he saw her now, which was nothing, and he thought of what she'd say to him now, which was nonsense. Toward the end of their marriage and toward the middle and even toward the beginning of the end of the beginning, she'd mostly talked a lot of gobbledegook. 'If the King of England says he'll love the Queen of England forever and then remarries, does he mean he'll love the first wife forever or whoever his wife is at the time?' she might ask. She fancied herself a Wittgenstein philosopher and often followed whatever she said with the phrase, 'That was *very* Wittgensteinian if I do say so myself, and I is who says I.' This had been during the Cuckold Period, as he now thought of it. In France, to be a cuckold was not to be pathetic. It was to be the star of a French film! And this was who he was in their marriage: a French movie star, never mind if they were living in Jersey, since you wouldn't specify *French* movie star if you were actually in France. Before the Cuckold Period, there'd been the Manifest Destiny Period, in which he believed he was accomplishing something greater than himself by settling down with her. (The children, the blessed unborn children!) And before that, there'd been the Great Awakening, in which he'd taught her a lot of things that he thought she'd like to know and which, she later told him, gently bored her. But that was Miranda. You just never knew with her.

For example, that she'd been with someone else.

Often when he was delirious, which was often, he wondered how he hadn't seen the signs. She'd said things like, 'When his expression is *genuine*, he has two identical faces.' He'd thought she was quoting – and she was – but also she was *meaning*, and what she'd meant was not that the philosopher had meant something incredible but that the philosopher had meant something pedestrian.

On good days, he could believe that that was exactly what he appeared to be: pedestrian, a pedestrian, a walker, walking, going places, on the ups, possessing two healthy feet at least. There'd been the book, seven, eight years before. He knew someone who assigned it at Montclair State in an intro course. But the things he did to women were not as cute to them as they had been thirty years ago. Some of the things were flirtation, and some of them were getting older. He needed his secretary to tell him the times the laundromat closed and the birthdays of his two sisters. He asked for help with the ratio of coffee grounds to water, referring tirelessly to this ratio as her secret recipe. 'And what if I wasn't around?' Clara would say.

'I'd die of heartache and weep rose petals,' he said.

'You talk the talk,' Clara said.

'But I don't walk the walk, I promise you.'

And it was true, he really didn't anymore. Once, he'd been attractive to his students. Now he was a man older than their fathers. They spoke to him kindly and loudly, and it depressed the hell out of him. Sometimes they brought him cookies cut in the shapes of candy canes or reindeer, as though he was so old he'd returned to a pre-prehensile state in which the id was driven by sugar rather than sex, and, oh God, didn't they know they could kill a prediabetic – his doctor's term – this way? Death by chocolate was more than an expression.

'Thank you very, very much!' one girl hissed through a smile on the last day of the semester. 'I learned a lot about the Protesting Affirmation, Professor Douglas!'

'I think you mean the Protestant Reformation,' he said.

'Yes!' the girl shouted more loudly. 'The Protesting Affirmation!'

It didn't even make sense, he thought bitterly; he hadn't lost any hair yet. In fact – that is, in the mirror – there was a significant – abundant, even – sprawl of the stuff, which he wore neatly combed over. So he told the mirror all the ways it was a ludicrous, vapid object with no soul or eyes; a parrot; monkey see, monkey do; a sorry wannabe if ever he'd seen one. He told it it was a mere proxy, and he told it it was a dime a dozen, though still a homewrecking slut. No, never again would he cry a hot tear for this mirror. Then when he was done berating the instrument of his own reflection, he sat down in his office chair to berate his young charges.

On his desk, typed stacks of pathetic blather towered. 'When Martin Luther King Jr posted the Ninety-Five Theses,' one paper began, 'black and whites were still not equal in rights in America. It took busses and courage to change the coarse of history and reformation.'

Douglas sighed. 'You're conflating centuries,' he wrote in the paper's margin. 'Be careful to remember the difference between the sixteenth century and the twentieth century!' He didn't even bother with the two Luthers. For thirty years his career had been reminding young people to be vigilant in their delineation of centuries, and the worst part was that he could never be fired anymore. Wasn't that the irony of it all? That you could be ousted from your *real* life, but not your public life?

But Miranda could not, after all, claim custody of Manhattan, and he would make a trip to the city on Christmas. It was bad enough she'd gotten tenure at the New School while he was stuck at Saint Peter's College in Jersey City, considering she hadn't even *had* a PhD when they'd first been married. He had loved the city first, just as he'd loved academia first, and he wouldn't be locked out this time. If he saw Miranda, he would think of something to say, and he would say it well. He would let her know what he thought of the New School (hippies, frauds) and tell her about all the holiday invitations he'd been forced to turn down what with the inconvenient finitude of time and all.

His sisters, kind, whitening women, had invited him to spend Christmas with them, their children and their grandchildren. Laura had two children and three grandchildren, one of whom was already ten. The other sister, Ramona, had one child and two grandchildren, and a lesbian partner whom she'd met at church thirteen years ago. Now her ex-husband and her lesbian partner and her child and grandchildren did things like have Ice Cream Sundae Funday Nights and veritable singalongs.

'Billy,' Ramona pleaded on the phone, 'you'll be all alone. Why do this to yourself – on *Christmas*? Don't you know you have family? Clarence is walking now. You haven't even seen his little baby walk.'

'But can he talk the talk?' Douglas tried to remember which one Clarence was.

'Talk?' Ramona was bewildered.

'You know, seduce, inveigle, slither into false intimacy?'

'Billy, have you spoken with Miranda recently or something? You sound awful,' Ramona said, 'again.'

Professor William Douglas coughed a little and made an excuse about a lozenge, then walked to the History office to see if anything particular was happening. If he wasn't by the phone, he wouldn't be lying when, eventually, he explained to Ramona that he'd missed her call. He might even run into Marlene, the boring little cutie from his night course. Sixty-two, and the thing that kept him functional was the possibility of running into minor crushes. Good God.

'I'm not making you more coffee,' Clara said.

Professor Douglas bowed. 'Happy holidays to you too.'

'Have you been drinking?' Clara sniffed.

'No,' he said, cupping his hand to smell his breath. He must remember to keep mouthwash in his office.

People in New Jersey talked about going to the city 'all the time'. 'If they're in New York all the time, then how can they be here now?' Miranda used to ask. 'I wish they *were* in New York all the time.' Douglas and Miranda had met and begun dating in the city. Back then, she was a young woman who enjoyed dressing beautifully for parties. Afterward, they'd return to their little one-bedroom apartment and undress beautifully. She was a legal assistant to an acquaintance of his, Robin Grubler, who had a tremendous unrequited affection for her.

'A tack!' Grubler would tell Douglas when he was drunk. 'Miranda is sharp. As. A. Tack.' It was the highest compliment he ever paid anyone and essentially equivalent to a statement of undying devotion. 'A tack,' he said, 'you dusty bastard.' Douglas had never understood what dusty was supposed to mean. He wasn't dusty. Maybe Grubler had said lucky. Maybe he was lucky.

Then a couple of years into the marriage, Douglas got an offer, and the offer was in New Jersey. Miranda complained about the food and accents, missing her job, loneliness. 'Oh, we used to live in Manhattan,' Miranda would explain to neighbors when she met them. 'We moved to New Jersey to make my husband's life easier.'

Sometimes, when she was depressed and unmedicated, he encouraged her to develop an inner life. What he meant was that it would be wonderful for her to have a place to retreat into too when the real world wasn't to her liking, so that he, her real-world husband, needn't talk her down into polite despair, which was the best he could do anyway. These talks, brief as they were, took him out of the sixteenth century when he should have been writing something about Luther that would recast the great Protestant himself as a rebel, sexy. Tenure, after all, wasn't guaranteed. But Miranda always wanted to visit with his sisters in Brooklyn. She became hysterical watching movies about the adventures of sassy secretaries. Sometimes when he was working through a manuscript, she stood by the doorway in her beautiful dinner clothes until he agreed to eat a meal with her. She was nothing like his first wife, a jazz musician, to whom he'd been married quite happily for ten days when he was twenty. Occasionally, he became so irritated that he had to masturbate to the thought of one of his students in his office after class, just to manage Miranda's antics at home with a smile. Finally, Douglas suggested she take a course in the city once a week, work on her relationship with herself. It sounded like something a sensitive husband would say to a sensitive wife.

But now, wasn't he the one working on himself – he, a man without a care in the world? It was just him and the entire run of human history – and his specialization once every four semesters when his elective course was offered. He didn't need to fix anyone except the only one he could. Which should be easy, but the city was a terrible snooze on Christmas. For a while, he walked through the East Village, and what was more awful than realizing that it was empty of actual counterculturalists was the reality that even the vomiting fraternity glutes were behaving well today, somewhere behind closed doors. He passed by a tattoo parlor, then a nail parlor, then a hair parlor. 'We're not hair today,' the sign said. 'Come back another dye.' It wasn't even witty. If they were going to be unavailable, they could at least be witty, like some of the women he'd pursued. 'A knock-knock joke is never clever,' he'd had to tell one girl he dated for a night. Then he'd added an addendum about street-crossing jokes before eventually giving up.

Beyond Tompkins Square Park and west a little, he was certain the city would indulge his fantasy. He didn't know what the fantasy was exactly, but he was certain he'd recognize it once it materialized and wasn't fantastical. He believed it had something to do with commerce or drinking or women, a feeling he thought he might have had thirty years ago. The feeling was that his words would land on someone and that that someone would respond in a way that the words landed back on him. He huddled inside his coat, walking purposefully, running almost, his face chilled pink. It wasn't so bad. The cold inspired character and briskness. Except in Stalinist Russia, of course.

A yellow cab slowed suggestively by the curb. Douglas raised his arm and jumped in quickly, then grabbed at his thigh.

'Where to?' the cabbie said.

'I think I pulled a muscle.'

'Bellevue Hospital? Is that Bellevue Hospital I hear?' the cabbie asked like an auctioneer.

'No, you're not listening,' Douglas said. 'Listen.' But he needed a moment to think. It had become increasingly difficult to remember which thoughts were his and which were his mind repeating those of Miranda. For years, ever since she'd enrolled in that ridiculous graduate program, he'd think of things she might say, then shoot them down within the privacy of his own mind. Lately, though, he forgot to shoot down her hypothetical speech. Its regularity matched his own thoughts. Rivalry could do that: confuse winning with a victory. In fact, he wondered whether Miranda hadn't ruined his previously above-average brain a little just by her presence, reciting her passages, exclaiming her Wittgensteinianness, though, of course, no one was Wittgensteinian except Wittgenstein, and even she had become un-Douglasian post hoc. But the cab driver was waiting for him to say something. They'd go nowhere unless he said something. His leg seized painfully when he rotated it in the hip socket.

'Almost there,' he said. He was on the brink of remembering someplace wonderful.

'Where?' the driver pointed a finger left and right expectantly.

'You know, *there*.'

A sigh from the front seat. 'So is that a yes to Bellevue?'

'Washington Square Park, please,' Douglas said to say something.

At Washington Square, there was hardly anyone to be seen walking around at all. A teenager ran shrieking down the street. Then he watched a woman with legs like pole-vaulting poles charge through a section of tamped-down snow in nothing but sandals and a cocktail dress. She didn't seem cold at all. For a moment, he thought he'd ask the girl if it wasn't painful to walk through snow in open-toed shoes. But what would that mean anyway? Miranda would say that even if he did take off his shoes and try walking sandaled through the snow himself, he wouldn't know what the girl meant by pain at all. Miranda would say it would be his pain, not hers, he was feeling. Miranda would do very kindly to get out of his head. And yet, wasn't she the person he was looking for on every street corner?

But she wasn't here wherever he had been that day. He'd walked around in the cold all day, and the only place he'd spent much time was a filthy little deli that smelled like mentholated cigarettes and halal food. The libraries were closed. The museums were closed. The shops were closed, and half the restaurants were too. He looked between the slats of blinds hanging in a twenty-four-hour diner window. Even this place, with its spongy shoestring fries and overpriced tuna salad, was closed for Christmas. Wasn't anyone Jewish anymore? he wondered.

'Is you racist or something?' said a man standing on the corner. He took a lollipop out of his fat little face with a loud suction sound just to say it. 'Ignorance is bliss.'

'I didn't realize we were having a conversation,' Douglas said.

'If you don't want to converse, don't talk,' the fat man said. He waved the spitty lollipop wildly, and blue sugar drool trickled from the corners of his mouth.

Douglas walked toward the train station. There was no reason to be here, and there never had been. He was always misinterpreting his own needs. It was half the reason he was in this mess. He thought of Miranda, how he'd wished she had an inner life when she had one already, a good one that stayed inside except for the occasional blue day. And now *that* Miranda, that life of hers, and also that life of theirs, was gone, replaced with ideas, and those ideas were not for the outer world. In fact, they were all ideas about the irrationality of interacting with it much at all. 'We identify a day as a Wednesday,' she might say. 'But what makes Wednesday Wednesday, not Tuesday or Thursday? And if I were to ask of a day whether it was a Wednesday, how would I prove it?'

'I'm not racist!' Douglas called to the candy man. '*I*, for one, know what day it is!'

'Thursday! I do too, bitch!' the candy man said.

'That's not what I meant,' Professor Douglas began to say. But what was the point? How would he prove it was Christmas?

In retrospect, the trip to the city had been a ridiculous idea. After all, the beginning of the beginning of the end had started on a trip to New York. On the train, he tried to engage Miranda with complaints about the departmental budget cuts, but all she wanted to talk about was this wonderful Wittgenstein she was learning about in her college course. '"Every sign *by itself* seems dead. *What* gives it life? In use it *lives*. Is it there that it has living breath within it? Or is the *use* its breath?"' she said, an eager sheen in her eye. 'Well?'

'I didn't think I needed to respond,' he said. 'It doesn't seem to have to do with real life at all.'

'Maybe when you say you didn't think you needed to respond, *you* didn't need to. Maybe *I* needed you to respond.'

'Is this still philosophy or do you just talk like that now?'

'Jesus, Bill.'

'What?' He looked at her looking out the window. From the side, her lips were two red jelly beans. He could absolutely bite them. This was real life: lips like jelly beans! Historical facts! He was a man of events, not ideas, a historian, a knower, not a philosopher. 'We'll be there soon,' he said.

'When is soon?'

'Twenty minutes.'

'That's not what I meant,' she said. 'When you imagine soon, the word soon, what do you see in your mind? When is it?'

'I feel like I can't say anything without it becoming a fucking discussion anymore,' he said.

'Lucky we're going to a play then,' she said. They didn't talk for the rest of the ride.

Now, when he groped at his memory, he was certain he could sense something that was almost a clue. But the more he tried to grab at the germ of their alienation, the less he knew what exactly the clue was. It just seemed that after that trip, nothing went right. He remembered one night she said was feeling a little sick on their way to a gallery opening in Chelsea. She told him she would drop him off before she went home, then kept her eyes closed the entire cab ride.

He'd assumed she really was sick, therefore settling on a dapper exit to cheer her. 'Promise you'll make sure my little girl gets home safe,' he said smarmily to the cab driver. It was a wry little joke that had always gotten a good-natured chuckle from a stranger the first time he was married.

But this time, the driver looked at him gravely. 'I promise you, sir: I will take care of your daughter.' Douglas tried to explain the irony – the husband, overprotective to the point of fatherliness, though of course he wasn't actually anyone's father – but the cab driver just kept saying, 'Your daughter is in safe hands, sir.' Later, when he came home, she pretended to be asleep, and the next day he couldn't make her admit her own pretense. Another time, they visited Ramona, and it was all a very nice afternoon until she began crying on the way back. He asked why she was crying. 'Because you don't know what I mean even when I mean what I say,' she said.

'When don't you mean what you say?' he asked.

'Sex,' she said.

It was January the second, and he'd managed to avoid his sisters and their offspring for the major winter holidays. The trip to New York had been disappointing, but the next semester was coming, and there were things to do, things to photocopy. He'd selected a new reading about the indulgence, redemption as a consumer item, the symbology of the forgiveness of sin. He would argue that the popularity of the indulgence itself revealed postmodern epistemological concerns. Then Ramona called, Ramona who was always self-improving, annoyingly enough, and had recently started trying to improve him too. He tried to bore her from fixing him, spoke about the chic new theories in history, which really weren't even all that new anymore.

'Happened is over. Happened has happened already,' he said, his voice cycling through octaves manically. 'Narrativity. Now *there's* something.' He didn't believe in these trendy theories, but with any luck Ramona would get tripped up on five-syllable words. His sister's lesbian partner could be heard humming in the background, as the ex-husband syncopated with a wooden spoon on a pot. Should it bother him that he couldn't remember the lesbian partner's name?

'But what the hay does narrativity have to do with *you*, Billy?' said Ramona.

It was a good question, actually. He sometimes did wonder what had happened to the form and thrust of his life. But the larger part of himself, the part that was hypothetically Miranda, was stuck on something he'd just said. 'Where is *there* when we say *there's something*?' he asked. 'For that matter,' he added, 'what do we mean by *is*, anyway?'

'Billy,' Ramona said. Her voice was rising with fear. 'Do you know what day it is? Do you know where you are? What's my name, Billy? Have you hit your head on something?'

He didn't know what day it was. 'I don't know, Sunday? That's really not a fair question during the recess, *Ramona*. R-A-M –'

Ramona told him he could stop spelling right now. Probably she wanted to go play the recorder. Her partner and ex-husband were still having a jolly time somewhere near the phone, or else very loudly. 'Anyway, I just thought you'd like to be included. That's the only reason I called.'

'Included in what?'

'In the new year's resolution. You stick to it better with a partner.'

'I don't have a resolution, though. I don't –' He paused. 'I don't resolve.'

Ramona cleared her throat. 'Well, maybe you should. Maybe you should work on your interpersonal skills. Like forgiveness.'

William Douglas closed his eyes.

'You should resolve things with Miranda, for example. Put yourself in her shoes. Anger is toxic waste to the soul, Billy. Do you want your soul to die, Billy?'

'I don't know why you think I have a soul, Ramona,' he said. 'I don't think *you* do.' It was difficult to know which was more irritating, preaching or pity. He avoided preaching and pitying equally, mostly because he was generally too delirious to do either. So, in fact, it was not that he avoided either. He was just too busy for them.

'You're just trying to hurt me now, Billy. That's not productive. When Andrea and I are angry with each other, we say, "Right now, I feel anger toward you, but I know that this is a temporary feeling." Then the other says, "I validate your feeling, and I also feel X."'

'X?'

'Yes, that's the fill-in-the-blank.'

'I'm not trying to hurt you. I don't think you can be hurt at all. I'm probably the only real person alive. That's what Miranda would want me to think, anyway. You see? I'm in her shoes. Her lousy philosopho-figurative shoes.'

'You're talking like a crazy person.'

'Exactly!' said Douglas. 'I'm talking like my ex-wife, the crazy person.'

'Billy, I feel anger toward you, but I know this is a temporary feeling.'

'X,' William Douglas said.

A man standing outside the strip mall and wearing tight yellow pants thrust a pamphlet at him. On the front, the words TURN YOUR GUT FROM GUTTER TO GLITTER appeared in red letters. Where had this man come from? Professor Douglas looked at the man's legs. To call them legs was to miss something of their fundamental meatiness, the striations and muscle weave. Why did you have to compare a thing to another to describe it? Nothing meant what it was supposed to anymore.

'By Day Ten the asshole starts blubbering mucus, and that's when you know your colon is immaculate as our savior Jesus Christ's conception,' the man told a woman wearing a bright pink parka. 'Take any sixty-something-year-old man and stand him naked by my side. Not only will he be more constipated, but ten times out of nine the triceps will hang like wet laundry in the wind.'

The woman was rapt. She had removed a small notebook from her purse and begun jotting notes.

'I cannot stress it enough: fiber fiber fiber! Do you think I chiseled my way down to 8 percent body fat with squat thrusts alone? Wake up, Terri Schiavo! This is science! And you, yes even you' – he pointed at Douglas – 'can follow my diet plan for a mere hundred dollars a month.'

'No thank you,' Douglas said, alarmed. 'I don't like science.'

'Don't like science!' The man in spandex was cheerfully bewildered. 'But science is everything!'

'Yeah,' the woman said. 'Science is the sun and the moon and the stars.'

'Ideologues on every corner!' Douglas shouted, though he hadn't meant to do more than think it.

'Did you just call us idiots?' the woman said. 'Because I'm in college, you know.'

'College!' Douglas walked quickly into the office supply store to buy something he needed but didn't remember anymore.

Toward the beginning or end of an aisle, he picked up a tape dispenser, then put it down. He touched gum erasers and thick résumé paper. But it was no use. Everywhere it was college students and language and ideas and betrayals. Every item in his life had been coded to evoke her. There she was in diet propaganda. There she was in the city. There she was in every word, smiling, as she said she was leaving him for someone who knew how to talk to her.

'Talk to you? What am I doing right now if I'm not talking to you?'

'Talking to who you think I was,' she said.

'It's not enough that you're sleeping with somebody else. Now you have to be pedantic?'

'But I'm not sleeping with someone else,' she said. 'Neil and I, what we have isn't sexual. I find him actually a bit ugly. But he's willing to think about what I think about. We have an ordinary language. He's with me.'

For a long time, Douglas had wished that he was the sort of man who could derive pleasure from the thought that Miranda was now with an ugly man. He could tell people that he used to be married to Miranda Shelby, the Wittgenstein scholar, and now she was with an ugly man. But the truth was, he didn't even understand what she meant by with her. He only knew what it meant to be without. And to be without her was to see her always, as if the very symbols of his misery had married themselves to the designs of life. It was for the world never to answer his pleas.

But should he see Miranda now, he would know finally what to say. If a man becomes better too late, he'd ask, was he worse than if he never got better at all? ∎

It was discovered that gut bacteria were responsible

It was discovered that gut bacteria were responsible
for human dreams. Each bacterium was entitled to pay
a fee in the form of mitochondrial energy to purchase
a 'dream token' to be dropped into a Potential Well. These
'tokens' were converted to synaptic prompts and transported
to the human brain in no particular order. So a 'token' for a
'baseball dream' deposited in the well when the human host
was aged 8 might only be used by the brain when the host
was 44, and this dream that might have been pleasant for an
8-year-old could instead emerge as a nightmare for a woman
on the brink of menopause who might worry about her
appearance in a baseball uniform, or who no longer recalled
how to hold a baseball glove and catch a ball in the field.

THE FLORIDA MOTEL

Kevin Canty

She sat on a tin chair outside of her room at the Florida Motel and thought about her children while she drank an iced tea. Her girl was thirty and had two children of her own now. Her baby boy was twenty-seven, an alcoholic in Olympia, Washington. Neither of them had time for Gertrude anymore, between the babies and the drinking. They had escaped, which she thought was probably as it should be. But most days she missed them.

The Florida Motel had started somewhere in the middle then gone far downhill. The swimming pool was half full, shopping carts poking out of the green water. The air-conditioning unit under her window was striped all the way down the front edge with burnt black lines where somebody had put a cigarette down to rest and then forgotten about it. Only the big neon sign, a green palm tree and the red letters FLORIDA, survived from when 441 was the busy highway through town and not a potholed backwater. Evening heat radiated off the beige concrete. Flattened swamp creatures lined the edges of the road: snakes, lizards, armadillos, possums.

Adele the maid came out of the office, dressed to go home in an orange tank top and cut-off jeans, barefoot. 'Y'all can go on up if you want,' she said. '215's empty now.'

'He checked out?'

Adele laughed. 'No,' she said, 'he never checked out. But he's gone. Three-in-the-morning gone. They got the key in the office.'

'Thank you.'

'You sure?'

'It's why I came here.'

'Well, good luck,' Adele said. 'Y'all crazy if you ask me but you didn't ask so good luck.'

Adele got into her Focus, blond hair in a cascade of wooden multicolored beads, and drove off trailing sparks from a dragging muffler pipe. Maybe she wasn't turning tricks after all, Gertrude thought. She would be driving a better car.

'You want to rent it or you just want to look around?' asked the manager.

'I just want to take a look,' she said. 'I can rent it if you want me to.'

'No, no,' said the manager, a small, sweaty man in a white shirt and with a rodent face. He seemed to be made nervous by her. He put the key on the counter so he wouldn't risk touching her. 'Go right on up,' he said. 'Take your time. As long as you like.'

'Why, thank you,' Gertrude said. She took the key and left, as glad to be rid of him as the manager was to be rid of her. Lately she alarmed people. She didn't know why and possibly didn't care.

Gertrude took the key to 215 up the stairs and along the second-floor balcony. The parking lot below was almost empty, cracked and oil-stained near the green rectangle of the pool. On the patio sat tin tables with attached metal umbrellas. She could sell them for a small fortune if she could get them home to Portland. They were Americana.

Gertrude was killing time. She didn't want to go into 215. Come all the way from Oregon and she couldn't bring herself.

She counted to eleven, a technique Bill taught her for jumping into cold water. The mind tricks itself, hesitates, plunges.

An ordinary ugly motel room.

Oh, she thought. Too much of a dream. Bill's last pictures. This slant of afternoon sunlight, through the curtains, onto the faded brocade of the bedspread. This knotty-pine desk with its cigarette burns, and through the open doorway – she knew before she saw it – would be a tiled shower stall with random tiles missing, like a message in code. An after-image, double exposure, a ghost in the room. Gertrude shivered, rooted in place, smelling the dust as it drifted through the yellow sunlight.

Bill had been her husband once, a long time before. He was a photographer and a drunk. The last pictures he ever took were here, in 215. He took pictures of the parking lot, the pool, of Adele the maid without her shirt on. He took pictures of everything. In his last days, he would pay strangers to drive him around and he would shoot roll after roll of Tri-X through the window of the moving car. When he died, he left behind 10,000 undeveloped rolls of film.

Left them to Gertrude, his ex, executrix.

There was really no reason for her to be here. Nothing but her own curiosity, which seemed morbid to her now. A long way for nothing. As the déjà vu faded away, she saw that she was in an ordinary rundown motel room, devoid of magic. A transient, public place, a bed that a thousand people had slept in. It was just an accident that Bill's life had ended here. It could have been anywhere. A room that was made for sleeping with strangers, or drinking alone.

Not just a regular bottle of vodka, either, but the big one, the kind with a handle. He drank the whole thing. Adele was the one who found him, a day after the fact, when he wouldn't answer her knock. A bottle, a body, a few dozen rolls of film. They shipped the film to her, along with his wallet, his watch, his battered Leica, a pamphlet of Catholic prayers. He carried pictures of their children in his wallet like any common salesman.

But had he meant to drink it all? A sober man would know that much alcohol was poison. But a drunk man wouldn't, necessarily.

No answers here. Gertrude sat on the edge of the bed with the sunlight falling across her legs. It was four o'clock. She had slept alone for several years now, or mostly so. She had lost interest, or had the interest beaten out of her. Men had worn her out.

Four o'clock on a hot afternoon.

The sound of slamming doors woke her out of her trance. The asphalt crew was home. They stood in the shade of the balcony, opening cans of beer and shouting insults at one another. *Ate up with the dumbass,* said one of them, and another replied, *Cocksucker.* Gertrude took one long last look around but the room was empty. She didn't even know what the question was.

She went to her room and changed clothes. The ones she had on felt dirty somehow, though the room had been slept in and cleaned a hundred times since then. She put on a red sundress with a low-cut neck and looked into her suitcase and thought fuck it and pulled her cowboy boots on. Ray-Bans and her hair tied back. She couldn't stand her hair in this kind of heat.

Purdy sat at one of the round tables on the patio, in the shade of the candy-colored metal umbrella, drinking a can of beer out of a foam rubber koozie that said FLORABAMA LOUNGE. He was the foreman of the asphalt crew, a big solid man in a dirty Panama hat and a short-sleeved shirt, untucked. The curve of his belly, the faint smell of diesel and sweat, even now, fresh from the shower. He reached into the cooler by his feet and handed her a dripping cold can of beer.

'What kind of day did you have?' Purdy asked.

'Oh,' she said, 'strange.'

'Did you get up into the room?'

Gertrude looked at him, trying to guess what she had told him on the bar stool the night before. More than she meant to. Drinking gimlets for Christ's sake.

'I was just up there,' she said.

'And?'

'And nothing,' she said. 'No clues. I thought that I would get a feeling or something, I don't know. It was kind of creepy walking in there, right at first. But after that, nothing.'

'Well, now you know,' said Purdy.

'This is his watch,' she said, holding out her left arm toward him. He took her wrist in one big hand and turned it this way and that.

'Nice watch,' he said.

And, yes, there was a kind of man who would always find her attractive and Purdy was that kind of man. Gertrude had blond hair which she was not about to give up – no natural grey for her – and the big tits that Bill had loved so. Maybe these days it took a little intentional blurring to make her pretty, an uncritical eye. It was all fading, all falling apart, bit by bit. But not yet.

'The other thing that was weird,' she said. 'I didn't see anything in the room or anything but I remembered when I was up there that the pictures he carried, the pictures of the kids? They were from way back, like early high school or middle school or something. They were already grown. But he'd kept the pictures from when they were little.'

'That doesn't seem strange to me,' said Purdy, and let go of her arm. 'I do the same.'

'Let's see them,' Gertrude said.

Purdy shot her a quick appraising look. He didn't seem to want to but he got his wallet out anyway: a pretty, skinny girl in glasses, about twelve or so, and a boy who looked like Purdy must have looked in high school, big but not soft, an athlete's crew cut. Some little warning bell went off in Gertrude's head but she ignored it.

'Where are they now?' she asked.

'Oh,' he said. Again, he didn't want to. 'Well, Sara's in college. Terry died a couple of years ago.'

'Oh, I'm so sorry. What happened?'

'In Afghanistan.'

'Oh, God,' she said. 'I'm sorry.'

'It was something he believed in,' Purdy said. 'So there's that.'

Gertrude could think of nothing to say. Purdy opened a cold beer and she sipped hers, already warming in the blood-warm afternoon. That's what Purdy called it, a coldbeer, all one word: get you a coldbeer?

'Goddamn it,' Purdy said. Then slammed himself upright. 'I'm going to go for a drive,' he said. 'You want to come along?'

'Where to?'

'Out in the country somewhere, I don't know. Away from here. You coming?'

'I guess,' she said. She wasn't sure she wanted to. That false sense of security, a big man like Bill, the same easy smile and blank eyes: she sat near Purdy and she felt the same ease and security as with Bill. She thought of his cock in his pants as if she had seen it, big like Bill's, a friendly thing. This was all wrong. She had no idea whether she ought to trust Purdy.

But the other option was the Florida Motel and so she found herself in the cab of his Toyota pickup, Tennessee plates and a cooler behind the seat, rolling down a country road in the half-light of the afternoon, AC blasting, live oaks on either side whose branches met over the road, Spanish moss, BOIL P-NUTS and holiness church signs. Purdy was still mad, still all closed up. Gertrude thought it wasn't fair. She was only flirting, in this new sad late-mid-life style: tell me about your kids, how crazy your ex was. Would Bill have said that? Would he have called her crazy?

No, Gertrude thought. She was the sane one, the bill-payer, diaper-changer.

Purdy said, 'Florida is a state for the simple-minded.'

'I thought you liked it here,' Gertrude said. 'Last night, you said you did.'

'You ever read about what's in the tap water down here?'

'I've yet to see you drink a glass of water.'

'It's not bad in January, when it's snowing back home. But no. The only time we get the work is dead of summer. People think it's a nice day because the sun is shining.'

'Go home, then.'

'I can't.'

'Why not?'

'I'll tell you later,' Purdy said, and relapsed into silent driving, thinking or brooding. Gertrude sipped her beer and watched out the window, the sand roads snaking back into dense greenery, black water, prehistory. In the passenger's seat again. Sometimes Bill would let her drive but not so often, not back then. She thought lovingly of her little Miata resting snugly in her Oregon garage. Nobody but Gertrude had ever driven that car. It was red. Most of the time, she thought, the loneliness was worth it.

They wound up at a restaurant on a lake, the sun still well above the horizon and blaring down onto the deck. Gertrude could not arrange the shade to suit her. She ordered gin to cool herself down. Purdy ordered a double Dickel on the rocks.

'Happy hour, babe,' the waitress said. 'They're all doubles.'

The waitress, too, wore an orange tank top, blond hair, tan leather skin, like most of the others on the deck, some kind of uniform. Maybe Purdy was right, a state for the stupid. Gertrude was certainly among strangers. She had gotten used to a certain kind of person back in Oregon, a polite, well-meaning, orderly person, but the people on this deck did not look to be any of these things. Suddenly she understood what she was doing here. She was among strangers, the place where Bill had chosen to spend his life. He was never good at home. He needed new and strange. And she needed to find him.

'See him?' Purdy said.

'See what?'

'Alligator,' he said. 'Right under the deck. You can just see his tail.'

Gertrude looked over the side and there it was, a black rubber thing with scales and points, right under her chair. If the deck gave way – and it certainly felt rickety enough – curtains for Gertrude. A little thrill.

'I went hunting for gators with a friend of mine once,' Purdy said. 'Middle of the night. Look for the eyes. You stand on the front deck of a flatboat going about thirty miles an hour and you try to spear 'em. Very exciting.'

Barbaric, she thought. She didn't say so.

Purdy said, 'One time. We were coming back home at four in the morning with a fifteen-foot gator in the back and it starts thrashing and rolling around, and the next thing you know, it's out on the grass strip next to the highway. Highway patrol comes up on us and we're standing there trying to get this thing back in the boat. He stands there laughing.'

'This is another being,' Gertrude said. 'You can't take pleasure in that.'

'He was dead already. Hit him in the head with a bang stick.'

'Then how was he moving?'

'They can twitch and roll around for a day or two. Just the way they're put together. A very primitive nervous system. Anyway, this cop goes back to his car and I thought maybe he had something that would help us get that big bastard back up in the boat, a come-along or something. But no. Comes back with a camera. Stands there laughing and taking pictures. Your tax dollars at work.'

A Mexican carnival, Gertrude thought. The waitress brought another round of drinks, unbidden. An arcade of life and danger, where Bill lived. She was there now. The sun inched down through the sky, toward a silhouette of primitive trees. Purdy ordered smoked mullet. Around her, middle-aged women in swimsuits slapped at bugs, while their husbands planned drug deals and house invasions. The mullet arrived, a brown slab of fish on a blue gas-station paper towel, dark with oil. It was delicious, especially with gin.

'But what isn't delicious with gin?' she asked Purdy. He seemed to know what she was talking about.

'Most places, this is bait,' he said. 'In Florida, it's food.'

It took her a moment to understand that he was talking about the mullet, which she'd thought was a haircut, until today.

'They've got gator on the menu here,' said Purdy. 'You ever eat gator?'

'Oh, why not?' she said, and next time the waitress came by with more drinks, Purdy ordered some, with French fries. Which is how you get a belly like that, she thought. So strict and practical! It was like a different language. Why not get a tattoo, if you were going to die young and pretty? But everybody here was too old to die young, and they still had the tattoos, sorry blue faded things.

'I've been thinking,' Purdy said. 'Your ex.'

'What about him?'

'He'd of known. When he went to the liquor store and bought that big bottle, he'd of known. It sounds like he'd been at it long enough.'

'I don't know,' she said.

His face was swimming in and out of focus, inner and outer, Purdy and Bill.

'It doesn't matter,' he said. 'It's not like day and night. You get to a point where it's going to be today or tomorrow, it's not a huge difference, you can see the end of the thing. At some point, you know, it's all about momentum. Give the devil a ride.'

'You never met him,' Gertrude said. 'You don't know what you're talking about.'

'Oh, I know what I'm talking about,' Purdy said. 'It was no accident.'

No, no, she was about to say. Then remembered: 10,000 undeveloped rolls of film. Something had come undone. It used to be all connected, when they were married, something about the drink and the work and the driving around. He'd go looking for trouble and then take pictures of it. All part of the same thing. But then some gear came loose. A Spaniard in the works.

'What if,' she said.

'What?'

'Never mind,' she said, and sipped her glass of gin, a glass full of silvery ice and magic. The sun was dipping down toward the horizon and as it did the drinkers rose to their feet and moved out toward the dock in ones and twos. Gertrude and Purdy were almost the last ones to follow. They stood watching as the sun's disk touched the horizon in a little notch between the trees, as it sank slowly out of this world and into the next. Gertrude thought of strangers awakening with the sunrise in another world, this world their dreamlife. Her and Purdy and all the others on the dock were characters in a dream on the other side of the world, things that needed to be expressed or worked through. The sun slipped lower and lower, a dome of orange light and then a slit and then, almost like a sigh, the sun was gone and the dense Florida night descended all at once. The drinkers on the dock all applauded and the Christmas lights lit up on the railing.

And that was it, pretty much. A few half-remembered moments: some driving, an argument, another bar. Some violent dream that a person on the other side of the world needed to have, some bad brain chemical, a residue of injury or accident. Purdy and Gertrude players on some unconscious stage.

She woke up in a lawn chair at dawn. Adele was shaking her gently awake. They were on the patio, next to the green pool, and the sky was an infinite no-color, no longer night, not yet blue.

Gertrude remembered throwing a shot glass at Purdy but she didn't remember why.

'I think I may have hurt myself,' Gertrude said.

'It's just a scratch,' Adele said, and they both looked at Gertrude's knee, parallel lines in dried blood, like somebody who had fallen through a rose bush. It didn't currently hurt, though it must have at some point.

'It's a big scratch,' said Gertrude.

'Let's get you tucked in,' said Adele. 'Catch your death out here.'

The beads in Adele's hair clacked and clattered as she led Gertrude across the lawn, which was not even real grass but some kind of sawtoothed weed. The white trucks of the asphalt crew were already gone. Early to rise, she thought. It was just six.

Inside, the one bed lay symmetrical and undisturbed under the coverlet, evidence, she hoped, that they hadn't slept together. The other bed, where her suitcase lay, was a mass of hurled and piled clothes, the leavings of some giant, crazed rodent, the beginnings of an ugly nest. Gertrude said, 'I feel stupid.'

'It's just a regular fuck-up,' Adele said. 'Everybody does sometimes.'

'I don't,' Gertrude said. 'I mean, really, I don't.'

'You've had a hard couple of days,' Adele said. Gertrude sat on the edge of the tidy bed and took her red boots off. Her feet were blistered and torn. When the air hit them, they began to hurt. She lay down on her back on top of the covers, like a funeral decoration, she thought. Feet together, arms crossed.

Adele picked up the yellow Kodak box from the messy bed.

'Are these his pictures?'

Alarms went off in Gertrude's head when she thought of the pictures, the naked ones especially. Some violation of trust, something like a lie, that Gertrude had seen Adele naked without her knowing.

'Can I look at them?'

'Sure,' said Gertrude, but she didn't feel easy. Even though Adele, of all people, would know how she posed. Gertrude sat up to watch the prints shuffle by, upside down. She had a man in Oregon named Tom Robinson develop the rolls of exposed film, a few at a time, and he would make contact sheets and they would go over them with a magnifying glass, circling the promising negatives with a white grease pencil. This was her year in that yellow box: the best of them, the sorting-out.

'These are, like, pictures of nothing,' Adele said, pausing at a view of the parking lot from the second-story balcony, just outside of 215. Then a picture of a girl holding an ice-cream cone and laughing.

'That's the idea,' Gertrude said. 'That's what he was trying to do.'

'People pay money for these?'

'There's a museum down in Arizona that wants to buy all of them. Everything. As soon as I'm ready to let go of them.'

Then came the pictures of Adele. She fanned them out across the tidy bed like a deck of cards. Gertrude couldn't tell if she was supposed to look at them but she was, Adele wasn't ashamed. As usual, these were his worst pictures: Adele looking wistful with her shirt off, staring out the window with one firm breast silhouetted against the light. Bill always needed to steal the picture. When somebody just gave it to him, the energy went out of it. Nothing excited him like the top of a stocking, a flash of panty under a windblown hem.

'These, I don't know,' Adele said. 'They're not bad. Not as bad as I was expecting when he took them.'

'He liked women,' Gertrude said.

'He liked to look at them, anyway,' Adele said. 'Can I have one?'

'As many as you want,' Gertrude said.

Adele pushed the ratpile of clothes a little off to the side and laid the pictures of herself out on the bedspread. She cracked the curtains to let the dawn light in, soft shadows. Then started to sort, a pile to one side, shuffling the prints around, putting the really difficult ones back in the box. She didn't like pictures of nothing. And then she didn't really like the ones of herself. One by one they shuffled back into the yellow Kodak box, until there was just one left, the girl with the smile and the ice-cream cone.

'It makes me happy just to look at her,' Adele said.

'You don't want one of yourself?'

'I've got a mirror,' Adele said. 'Now you get yourself some sleep.'

'OK.'

'And thanks for coming. I would have always wondered.'

Adele took her print and quickly darted in and kissed Gertrude on the forehead and left. So that's what I was doing here, Gertrude thought. She had been wondering. She slipped between the scratchy sheets, thinking that she was done now, she could let go, the museum down in Arizona could have them and she could have her life back. So sleepy! She closed her eyes and felt the weight of sleep pressing down on her. When she woke, at noon or so, she'd leave the Florida Motel, drive her little rental car to the Jacksonville airport and back into her world. But that was later. Now it was time to sleep.

Gertrude slipped away. Somewhere on the far side of the world, a dreamer was about to wake up with a faint, fogged memory, a colorful dream that she will try to touch, try to fix in her mind before it dissipates into the waking air. ■

TRACES II

Ian Teh

THE SOURCE

Ngoring Lake
Sanjiangyuan National Nature Reserve, Qinghai, China, 2014

In the 1990s, China's Yellow River began to dry up, and in 1997 it failed to reach the sea for several months. In an effort to address the problem, government officials launched a scheme to protect the river's source, a region called Sanjiangyuan (Three River Source) in north-west Qinghai Province, also home to the sources of the Yangtze and Mekong rivers. The Sanjiangyuan National Nature Reserve was established in 2000. Since then, Ngoring Lake, the largest of the lakes in the reserve, has seen its water levels rise and is now larger than its historical average. Local officials claim this is proof that the government's environmental preservation efforts have been successful, but recent research suggests a more worrying explanation: climate change.

Mountain Range
Anemaqen, Qinghai, China, 2014

Millions of people get their water from the great rivers linked to the Tibetan plateau. This land mass has an average elevation of more than five thousand metres, 80 per cent of which is covered in permafrost. It governs the Asian weather system, with its lakes, glaciers and wetlands acting as a huge water tower. Scientists call it the 'third pole' because of its influence on the earth's climate. Over the past forty years, the plateau has been warming much faster than the rest of the world, at a rate of 0.5 degrees Fahrenheit per decade. By some estimates, this has caused up to a fifth of the permafrost to melt.

Grazing Yaks
Gyaring Lake, Qinghai, China, 2014

The Tibetan plateau covers all of the Tibet Autonomous Region, much of
Qinghai Province and parts of Sichuan Province, stretching for 965,000
square miles, an area larger than Alaska, Texas and Nevada combined. In the
1970s, the communal system of open pastoral grazing that had existed for
centuries on the plateau began to change. Grasslands began to deteriorate.
Around the same time, economic reforms led to the privatisation of formerly
communal lands. Fencing altered the grazing patterns herders had used to
move their livestock over the fragile landscape. Confined to smaller areas, the
animals overgrazed, further damaging the grasslands.

New Residential Development
Guide, Qinghai, China, 2014

Approximately three hundred miles north-east of Ngoring Lake, in an as
yet uninhabited residential development, Tibetan nomads let their herds
graze the small patches. In 2003, the Chinese government implemented the
programme *tuimu huancao*, meaning 'retire livestock and restore grassland'.
Since 2006, as many as two million people have been relocated in an effort to
restore grasslands and forests, a process the government calls 'environmental
migration'. Since the introduction of *tuimu huancao*, studies have shown that
the government relocation efforts have more to do with economic policy than
restoration or protection of the delicate ecosystem.

Road Construction
Golog Tibetan Autonomous Prefecture, Qinghai, China, 2014

Over the past decades, as China's cities and economy have grown rapidly, the Sanjiangyuan National Nature Reserve has been increasingly explored for resource extraction. A single mine, the Muli mine, contains 3.5 billion tons of coal, or 87 per cent of the province's reserves. The infrastructure necessary to move supplies and resources has further altered the landscape as road-construction projects cut through the plateau and open mining pits abut protected wilderness areas.

Abandoned Five-Star Hotel Construction
Guide, Qinghai, China, 2014

One of the benefits of creating the reserve, according to China's State Council,
would be 'ecological protection and construction' on the plateau. Development,
however, soon extended to mining and real estate. Meanwhile, some of the
tourism-related projects have been lost to changing political winds: according
to a local security guard, construction of this five-star hotel came to a halt
when developers couldn't secure the necessary permits after a turnover in
local government personnel. Scientists have raised concerns that large towns
and cities, and the infrastructure that connects them, will inevitably increase
the stress on the local ecology.

THE MIDDLE REACHES

Cityscape
Lanzhou, Gansu, China, 2011

Since 1949, Lanzhou, once a Silk Road trading post, has morphed from the capital of a poverty-stricken province into the heart of a major industrial area. The largest and first city on the Yellow River, it is the centre of the country's petrochemical industry and a key regional transport hub between eastern and western China. Among the country's 660 cities, more than four hundred lack sufficient water, while more than one hundred suffer from severe shortages. According to recent reports by the Chinese government and international NGOs like the Blacksmith Institute, Lanzhou is China's most polluted city and one of the thirty most polluted cities in the world.

Desert
Baiyin, Gansu, China, 2011

A man from an illegal mine walks on a dirt track leading out of the mountains. Desertification in the region is a serious problem, consuming an area greater than that taken by farmland. Nearly all of China's desertification occurs in the west of the country and approximately 30 per cent of the country's surface area is desert. China's rapid industrialisation, overgrazing and expansion of agricultural land accelerate the advance of deserts, which are now swallowing up a million acres of grassland each year.

Landfill Construction
Hejin, Shanxi, China, 2011

Workers unroll sheets of plastic to line a new landfill. Just over a generation ago, refuse was rarely a problem because families, then largely poor and rural, used and reused everything. As cities have grown, urban support systems have been unable to keep up with the growing demand for the processing and disposing of waste. Most landfills are poorly managed and have only thin linings of plastic or fibreglass. These sites leach heavy metals, ammonia and bacteria into the groundwater and soil, and the decomposing waste sends out methane and carbon dioxide.

Quarry and Temple
Baiyin, Gansu, China, 2011

Quarries producing limestone, used for construction and as flux for the process of steel-making, are among a number of common features found in industrial towns. Heavy industry in this area has meant a high consumption of coal and water. Based on current figures, it is estimated that the 2015 development of the coal industry in the west will consume up to 10 billion cubic metres of water, approximately a quarter of the annual flow of the Yellow River.

Banks of the Yellow River
Hejin, Shanxi, China, 2011

A couple sits by the only remaining undeveloped section of the river. Although China has roughly the same amount of water as the United States, its population is nearly five times greater, making water a precious and increasingly sought-after resource. The heavily industrialised area around Hejin contains some of the most polluted waters in the river. In 2007, the Yellow River Conservancy Commission stated that one third of the river system had pollution levels that made the water unfit for drinking, aquaculture, agriculture or even industrial use.

TRACES II

From 2006 to 2010, I photographed the coal industry in China and its impact on the western hinterlands of the country. One body of work, *Traces I*, was a series of landscapes, often devoid of people, that beneath their neutral surfaces harboured highly politicised histories and revealed physical traces of change caused by human intervention. *Traces II*, which I began in 2011, is an extension of that study, with a particular focus on the Yellow River.

Few rivers have captured the soul of a nation more deeply than the Yellow River. Historically a symbol of enduring glory, a force of nature both feared and revered, it has provided water for life downstream for thousands of years. Its environmental decline underlines the dark side of the country's economic miracle, and is a tragedy whose consequences extend far beyond the 150 million people it directly sustains. There are often appropriate initiatives and legislation to protect the environment and its people, but these are systematically overlooked as the ambitions of the state are prioritised over the rule of law. My photographs offer clues to the incremental everyday changes that we fail to notice in the drive towards advancement and in the hectic minutiae of our daily lives. They attempt to show what happens when an area that was largely rural becomes increasingly urban and industrial, and to reveal the costs of rapid development on the communities beyond the river's immediate surroundings.

By depicting these landscapes as predominantly beautiful, almost dreamlike, I seek resonance with some of the romantic notions about this once great river. The search is for a gentle beauty, but also for muted signs of a landscape in the throes of transition. I am interested in the dissonance created between the ambivalent images and the historical, economic and scientific narrative that accompanies them. My hope is that together they connect viewers to the front lines of climate change, where the environmental crisis under way, like climate change itself, isn't always easy to see. ∎

GRANTA
THE MAGAZINE OF NEW WRITING

PRINT SUBSCRIPTION REPLY FORM FOR UK, EUROPE AND REST OF THE WORLD
(includes digital access). For digital-only subscriptions, please visit granta.com.

GUARANTEE: If I am ever dissatisfied with my *Granta* subscription, I will simply notify you, and you will send me a complete refund or credit my credit card, as applicable, for all un-mailed issues.

YOUR DETAILS

TITLE ....
NAME ....
ADDRESS ....
POSTCODE ....
EMAIL ....

☐ Please tick this box if you do not wish to receive special offers from *Granta*
☐ Please tick this box if you do not wish to receive offers from organizations selected by *Granta*

YOUR PAYMENT DETAILS

1) ☐ Pay £32 (saving £20) by Direct Debit

To pay by Direct Debit please complete the mandate and return to the address shown below.

2) Pay by cheque or credit/debit card. Please complete below:

1 year subscription: ☐ UK: £36   ☐ Europe: £42   ☐ Rest of World: £46

3 year subscription: ☐ UK: £99   ☐ Europe: £108   ☐ Rest of World: £126

I wish to pay by ☐ CHEQUE   ☐ CREDIT/DEBIT CARD

Cheque enclosed for £ _____ made payable to *Granta*.

Please charge £ _____ to my: ☐ Visa ☐ MasterCard ☐ Amex ☐ Switch/Maestro

Card No. ☐☐☐☐☐☐☐☐☐☐☐☐☐☐☐☐

Valid from *(if applicable)* ☐☐ / ☐☐   Expiry Date ☐☐ / ☐☐   Issue No. ☐☐

Security No. ☐☐☐

SIGNATURE .... DATE ....

Instructions to your Bank or Building Society to pay by Direct Debit

BANK NAME ....
BANK ADDRESS ....
POSTCODE ....
ACCOUNT IN THE NAMES(S) OF: ....
SIGNED .... DATE ....

DIRECT Debit

Instructions to your Bank or Building Society: Please pay Granta Publications direct debits from the account detailed on this instruction subject to the safeguards assured by the direct debit guarantee. I understand that this instruction may remain with Granta and, if so, details will be passed electronically to my bank/building society. Banks and building societies may not accept direct debit instructions from some types of account.

Bank/building society account number

☐☐☐☐☐☐☐☐

Sort Code

☐☐☐☐☐☐

Originator's Identification

9 1 3 1 3 3

Please mail this order form with payment instructions to:

Granta Publications
12 Addison Avenue
London, W11 4QR
Or call +44(0)208 955 7011
Or visit GRANTA.COM for details

FREE ENTRY

WITH REGISTRATION
ON WEBSITE

Z
ZEE
ENTERTAINMENT

JAIPUR
LITERATURE
FESTIVAL

21st-25th January
2016

THE WORLD'S LARGEST FREE LITERARY FESTIVAL

AS THE LARGEST FREE LITERARY FESTIVAL ON EARTH, THE ZEE JAIPUR LITERATURE FESTIVAL BRINGS TOGETHER SOME OF THE GREATEST THINKERS AND WRITERS FROM ACROSS SOUTH ASIA AND THE WORLD.

From Nobel laureates to local language writers, Man Booker prize winners to debut novelists, every January the most remarkable, witty, sensitive and brilliant collection of authors come together for five days of readings, debates and discussions at the beautiful Diggi Palace in the Rajasthani capital Jaipur.

FOR MORE INFORMATION
jaipurliteraturefestival.org

The author's mother Widad, with her firstborn daughter Siham
Courtesy of the author

MOTHER'S HOUSE

Raja Shehadeh

One can never be sure whether one is doing the right thing, especially when the patient, like my mother at the end, can only speak with difficulty. But all indications were that she did not care to go on living.

How quick is the deterioration when it starts, how quick the descent into oblivion.

That morning my brother Samer, my wife Penny and I went to my mother's flat to say our goodbyes, and to empty it. I had expected it would be a cold house, without life. The house of my parents, the house of the middle years – years of living a middle-class life that was also so turbulent, troubled and full of tragedy. The house of so many dramas, long past and more recent, from which both my parents were carried out in coffins. When we have emptied it we will be giving up this house, which Mother didn't own, and I will never again have to see anyone carried out from it. But as it turned out we didn't find the house so lifeless. My father and mother were still there, as was more of myself than I expected.

Evening had descended now, twilight was over, night was upon us – a dark moonless night. I walked to Mother's room, where I saw the quilt spread on her empty bed, that same quilt that had accompanied my parents in every house they'd ever lived in.

A few months before Mother died, my brother called. 'Do you think she can recognise us?' His voice betrayed sadness, disappointment and a profound wrenching hurt. I said I didn't know.

Just a few weeks earlier she had been able to recite Mark Antony's speech from *Julius Caesar*, which she had studied at the Anglican School for Girls in Jerusalem. It was as though she was emerging from behind the veil of death to prove to us that she had not lost her mind. She was making the decision to leave this life with her mind intact. It was a valiant, dignified act that proved that in choosing to die she was still exercising her will. She was fed up with life.

The process of deterioration, the progressive descent, had been going on for a while. My heart fell when I noticed that my mother had not been cleaning her teeth. When she was well she never failed to do this. We were also getting accounts from her helper of Mother waking up at night and walking through the house calling for my father: 'Aziz, Aziz, where are you?'

The light coming into the house was making shadows. It was the hour Mother hated most, when she did her best not to be alone.

Mother always said, 'The moment the neighbour rang the doorbell and I heard the fear in his voice I knew what had happened.' It was as though she had been expecting it. That moment was never forgotten. It marked the transition from having a husband and being a proud wife to becoming a miserable widow.

Later, her friend Ibtisam, who lost her own husband a while back, would boast, speaking rapidly without pausing for breath, that it had been her husband, the medical doctor, who was the first to arrive at the scene of the crime. She would proceed to enlighten my mother about what her husband saw when he arrived at the driveway of the garage, where my father had just parked his car and was making his way to the door of the building. How my father, whose throat had been slit by that murderer, lay in a pool of blood that spilled all the way down to the street. And how the doctor had put his fingers to my father's throat to check whether there was any pulse but found him already dead. It was too late to do anything for him.

After he was gone we would sit, my mother and I, in the sunroom. Mother would ask imploringly, 'Why did he do this?' As if he did it to himself. Mother had that habit, of blaming the victim. I would say that he lived as he wanted. He satisfied himself. This is how he wanted to live.

'But to have left me like this?' And I would be unsympathetic, unable to begin to understand the nature of their relationship, which I got completely wrong. I could not appreciate that as a woman of her generation she was tied to and completed by her man and had no life independent of him.

'Why?' she would say. 'What was it all for? What more did we need? Why did he have to keep on fighting? Who for? Who deserves all this struggle? Who cares about me now? Now that he's gone and left me alone what sort of life do I have? It galls my heart.

'When he was alive our house would be full of supplicants, those who wanted him to intercede on their behalf with the military rulers. They put him forward, exposed him to danger while they hid behind him, fearing to tarnish their own names. He went ahead while they remained concealed. He was always willing to help anyone who asked, as long as he could. The people who asked for his help never appreciated what it took out of him and what it cost me, seeing him suffer as he did from fatigue and incrimination. He never gave up. If it was an official he needed to contact to get the work done, he would call again and again, twenty, thirty, forty times if necessary, never giving up. He would be more adamant than the person needing the favour. It was a question of pride. He never allowed himself to fail, whatever the cost. Where were all these people after he was gone?'

I was aware that he had done a lot for us as well. He kept us feeling special and dignified and saved us from suffering the worst of the defeat and the terrible situation under occupation. He stood up to the occupier and was able to face the soldiers and their officers at every point. He never submitted to them.

At the press conference we held at the American Colony Hotel in Jerusalem to report on the failure of the Israeli police to carry out a proper investigation into his murder, my mother had said, 'The man who did the most for peace is left to die without justice.' But this fell on deaf ears. She was addressing the Israeli public, among whom were many friends of hers, but not one of them called her to offer assistance.

She was right to be angry. After he died everyone abandoned her. Our people crept back to their small holes, preferring not to stick their necks out or speak about it, many feeling ashamed of the implication of their leaders in this murder. The Israelis, smug in their own way, said, 'Well, of course this is what it's like for those, however decent they might be, who live on the other side.'

And how brave she was when we went on our quest for justice together. It was her last service, last sacrifice, to a husband who required so much from her throughout their life together. But we could not succeed. They closed all the doors in our faces. She refused to see him after he died, saying she wanted to remember him energetic and active, not as a corpse. She never visited his grave and hardly ever talked about him. He was there in her life, accompanying her in silence. She never gave him up. It might be that Mother's refusal to leave the house where the murder happened was out of her sense of allegiance to her husband. She remained there, a custodian of the house, of Father's possessions and papers, refusing ever to abandon her post.

As we moved about the house today we found more and more evidence of this, more and more of their life together. Father's side of their closet was still packed full with his clothes. She never gave them away. Everything in the house indicated that she was waiting for him to return. She could not accept that he was gone.

I looked at the TV room with its large round coffee table over the Persian carpet, now covered with boxes of Father's papers and books, blocking the passage, and thought of him moving so briskly, so energetically around the house.

'Mama, why don't you open your eyes? Is it painful for you to do it?' I asked her.

'No,' she answered. Then added, in a matter-of-fact tone, 'I want to finish.'

It was not the first time that she used the word 'finish' in English. Earlier, Penny and I had been talking to her about Jaffa, to cheer her up.

In the last years of her life she was tense, anxious and unhappy most of the time. The only time she cheered up was when we took her to Jaffa to sit by the sea. This was the one instance when she asked for a cigarette and she smoked it with great pleasure, blowing the smoke up into the air with a sense of abandon.

'Mother,' I asked during that last week of her life, 'would you like us to take you to Jaffa to sit by the sea and smoke a cigarette?'

'No. Finish,' she said. It had become an effort for her to articulate words and this was all she could come up with.

I had been suspecting it, but after this I felt certain that for the past several weeks my mother had been wanting to die. Perhaps she thought that if she closed her eyes, if she shut off the world, it would happen.

Penny did not agree. 'Her body is responding. If she had really decided to die she would not eat.'

'But then she is only eating,' I said, 'because she is being fed and doesn't want to refuse and get into the hassle of having us urge her to do it; she is in a passive mode and just wants to finish with it.'

If I had the courage and knew how, I would have helped her do it. It would have been the kindest thing to do.

I knew it. I knew that Mother was fighting for death. Fighting to die. Trying to prepare herself to face what was coming. As always she did this her way. She did not express emotions; she kept it all to herself. I hovered around. Not untypically she made me feel inadequate. If I were a good son, I thought, I would help her die. This was what she wanted most of all and I could, if I had the courage, lend a hand. But I didn't have it in me. It is so like my mother – even in death – to leave me feeling guilty, inadequate, not quite the man she had hoped I'd be.

And yet, Mother never mentioned death until the last months, when it hit. She was obviously readying herself. One day, a month before she died, her helper reported that when Mother got up in the morning feeling a bit better she told her, 'Death seems to have passed me by.' I fear she didn't sound triumphant.

She stopped being a mother and became a woman preparing to die, seeking help for it from those who had preceded her – her father and mother. She was their child again and kept on calling them each in turn to come be with her, to come to her rescue. She now needed them above anyone else.

Penny and I made several attempts to wake her up, urge her to return to us. But she had decided to follow a man with a white beard who seemed to be culled out of her rich imagination full of elves and the strange characters that inhabited the mysterious forests in the amazing stories she told me when I was a child. Now she was giving herself up to that man, following him deep, deep into the mystical forest about which we were ignorant.

She would no longer move about the house at night calling her husband, looking for him in every room. 'Aziz, where are you? Where are you?' She was going to join him in death. She would have to go alone down that last dark alley to the damp forest, following that white-bearded man with white hair and a dangling white beard, who wore a sky-blue jacket with many pockets and who had been bidding her to come. His long face with blue eyes bidding her to come, come to him. Reluctantly she began to follow. Her cheeks hollowed. Her face grew longer. She started looking different, more of the other world than this one.

I looked out at the horizon from the glass veranda and thought of her during those last few weeks, facing the end of her life on earth, and it occurred to me that the question of whether or not she would be returning must have been connected in her mind with whether there was something to return to. She must have decided there wasn't, and so she continued forward, never turning back.

How bravely she approached death. This was her final lesson to me: not to worry about it. When it comes you'll be ready. As I stood there looking into the dark, the words of my father came back to me. Words that he had said twenty-five years earlier as we sat around the white-painted wooden table in the kitchen: 'You'll take care of your mother when I'm gone,' he had said. Did I? Have I fulfilled my promise? Have I been a good son?

I kept a diary of the last months of Mother's life. But it is far too sad to reread. It speaks of my repeated attempts to have her die in the house, away from the hospital she hated. But even in that I failed her. It is very hard to know, in the case of a dying parent, what the best choices are, medically and ethically. And one has very little help. I rode with her in the ambulance that last time, hearing her cries of pain, which were now muted. She had so little energy, even for that.

How painful it was for me to see my mother in hospital, pricked by all those needles, suffering pain from treatment she did not want because by that point she had decided she wanted to die. A week later she died in hospital with the needles still pricking her arms and lovely hands and an oxygen mask over her beautiful mouth, preventing her from speaking even if she had wanted to. We stood around, unable to help in any way.

My brother Samer had by now done most of the work of emptying the house. It had all been boxed, the entire household reduced to boxes. This is how life ends, I thought, in a box and down into the earth. But before I started on my final tour of the house as it was dismembered and the walls denuded, there were still a few things with particular meaning that we had to decide about.

The first was the portrait of Father painted by Ismail Shammout during my father's exile in Rome. As the older son it should go to me. But since I have no children I offered it to my brother. When it came to the porcelain Buddha that my parents had brought with them from their home in Jaffa, Samer offered it to me because I had written about it in one of my books. But I gave it back to him. It has to stay in the family and he is the one who can ensure that it will.

Then we got to the last painting on the wall, the one by Mother's aunt Lora, of a woman with a broken jar. Her son Suheil had asked me to send it to him in London, where he now lives. As I removed it from its frame, dust came out. It was Haifa dust from the convent where the painting was kept until we managed to retrieve it after 1967. The dust flew up hesitantly and then disappeared. I realised it was the last physical link that we had to that old land where my parents' generation had once lived, a puff of old dust.

As Samer was removing the portrait of Father from the wall I remembered what Mother had said when I tried to use the presence of the portrait to prove to her that this was her house – in her last few months of life she refused to believe that it was. 'They come every night and place the same things on the wall, this is why it is here,' she had said. 'But this is not my house. I want to go home.' And here we were, as predicted, removing it from the wall.

All too quickly the walls were bare, and the old familiar furniture was removed and the books packed. The space between these walls was growing narrower; it was ceasing to be her house or indeed the house of my youth.

We had piled up the clothes to give away. Before we left them, I looked for the black jacket she was fond of and wore so often for many years. I held it to my nose and smelled it, the last whiff of Mother's scent.

As I left the emptied house I saw one of the remaining relics of her old conventional life, standing silently at the window in the dark, hoping that she would not be seen by us, pretending not to be home and so be excused from having to perform the neighbourly and friendly duties towards us, the children of her lifelong friends and neighbours. As I looked at her made-up face, I felt glad to be leaving forever a life where maids did the laborious work, where concern was paid to who invites whom and who gets invited to which parties.

A social circle of vacuous people who cling together not because they really care for one another's company but because they cannot stand to be alone, people I never cared for – perhaps not unlike my grandfather Salim, who preferred to stay alone in his room, reading his books while his wife Julia socialised – but to whom I remained tied through my mother and her suffering in later years at being excluded and shunned by them.

It was appropriate, I thought, not to have to say goodbye, or to meet this neighbour, but rather to turn my back silently and definitively on the social conventions of this meek society, so full of affectation, which I would never again have to bother with, think about or tolerate. Without her put-on smile, Mother's neighbour looked both sad and severe.

I said my final, silent goodbye to Mother's house and, laden with boxes, walked away to my car through the garage where the dreadful deed that had destroyed her life was perpetrated.

A few months later I was in my study when Penny came in. 'Don't you want to put up a picture of your mother?' she asked, and brought me a few to choose from.

I had thought about it but was not sure I was ready to turn my mother, who lives on so strongly in my mind, into a framed picture on the shelf. But I looked at one picture and then another and another from the pack that Penny had brought for me to choose from. They were not from the sad and difficult period that has persisted in my mind, but from a happier time when she looked radiant, and I remembered that she had enjoyed better times and her life had not been all gloom and misery. I chose one in which I thought she was looking happy.

Now when I look more closely at her smiling face I notice what had eluded me for so long. Even though the mouth has a valiant wide smile, I realise that the eyes tell a different story. They are focused on the distant past. They do not express happiness. The smiling mouth is a distraction, the public face, the joy she wanted to put on to please others. It is her eyes that speak of her mood at that point in her life. They belie what is expressed by the mouth. Yet despite her many difficult ordeals she had always tried to keep on smiling even when for so many years her sadness and pain were overwhelming. Sometimes she couldn't manage it and I was overcome by despair and did not know what to do. At the end her pain and sorrow took over and she was taken away from us.

I look again at the framed photograph and decide that I shall follow her lead. I will do what she did during her lifetime and concentrate on the smile. ■

Granta Books congratulates its authors on the 2015 Folio Prize Shortlist

Ben Lerner,
10:04

Jenny Offill,
Dept. of Speculation

Yvonne Adhiambo
Owuor, *Dust*

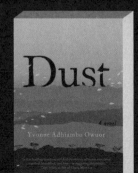

GRANTA

© BENJAMIN LOWY
from *Iraq* | *Perspectives 1: Windows*, 2003–2008
View from an American Army Humvee
Abu Ghraib, Iraq, 9 July 2007

AFTER ZERO HOUR

Janine di Giovanni

I

In the last days of Iraq, shortly before the collapse of Saddam Hussein's regime, the Ministry of Information, which controlled the movements of all the press, granted my request to travel the country by car.

That was in 2002. My companions on these long and melancholy trips – shadowed by the coming American invasion – were my driver, Munzer, a transplanted Palestinian Sunni whose family had emigrated to Iraq in 1948, and my translator, Reem, who came from Babil Province. Sometimes we were accompanied by a bad-tempered 'minder', graciously provided by the ministry, whose purpose was to spy on us and take detailed notes about where we were going and whom we saw.

Occasionally Ali, another translator, a film scholar who worshipped Martin Scorsese, also came along. But he and Munzer had a tumultuous relationship, which sometimes came close to blows, so we tried to keep them separated.

Munzer had a 1987 Oldsmobile, like something out of *Starsky and Hutch*. I would load the car with fruit and water, a medical kit and emergency supplies, and we would begin, driving up and down, north and south, east and west, across the country.

I knew then, even as we were traversing the endless Saddam

Hussein highways – Baghdad to Basra, Baghdad to Mosul – that I would never take those routes so effortlessly again in my lifetime.

With the invasion, and the insurgent war that followed, Iraq would virtually disappear. The land of date trees, oasis and desert would be marked by checkpoints and graves.

I did not know then the extent of the anguish that would fall on this beguiling place, known as the land between two rivers – the Euphrates and the Tigris – but I did know as we drove through those biblical ruins, those languid farming villages, those dusty cities, that they would be closed forever after the bombs started falling.

The American invasion was planned and even had a date, but there was little solid information about it. We were cut off from the world on those trips. The Internet in Baghdad was carefully controlled, and there was no cell-phone service. I did have a smuggled satellite phone, but it was illegal to use it. The Mukhabarat, the secret police, watched us so closely that it would have been impossible to go outside, find a satellite in the sky and set it up without being caught. I kept it for near emergencies.

Occasionally Reem and I would watch Iraqi TV, but mostly we talked to people and got immersed in local gossip, the rumours and paranoia that inevitably come with the end of a regime. It was an overbearingly tense and claustrophobic time: a great sense of doom hung in the polluted air.

'What will happen when the Americans come?' I asked Reem, or Ali. In Baghdad, children were digging trenches and sandbags were being piled on street corners, but no one wanted to look too far ahead. Reem usually stayed silent. Once, Munzer answered: 'We will fight!' and that was that. We kept driving.

We drove to the sacred Shia cities of Najaf and Karbala, we drove to Saddam's home town of Tikrit, we drove to Samarra and Babylon and Diyala. We spent Eid, the festival marking the end of Ramadan, with a farmer who proudly slaughtered a goat in front of us in an alleyway – a gruesome killing, and then lunch. Once, Reem and I went to the Imam Hussein shrine in Karbala. Reem went inside and came back with a green ribbon for me. 'It means,' she said solemnly, 'you get a wish.'

Reem knew what I wanted. I was getting married in August, and I dropped my head and closed my eyes and wished that I would be happy, would be safe, and that we would have a healthy child.

Along the way on our long days, we met Iraqis from the sects and tribes that made up the extraordinarily diverse ethnicities of the country. We went to stay with the Yazidis and with blue-eyed Assyrians; we met Sunni Arabs, Shia Arabs, Turkmen, Chaldeans, Circassians, Armenian Iraqis, Iraqi Jews and Kurds.

We knelt with terrified Christians celebrating Mass a few days before Christmas in Mosul, praying for the war to be halted. A few months later, on Ash Wednesday, we sat with some Chaldeans at St Mary's Church on Palestine Street in Baghdad, which in 2009 would be blown up by a bomb as worshippers were leaving.

It was surreal to be poised, waiting for war to start. The city was suddenly invaded with international do-gooders who showed up in a last-ditch attempt to stop the bombing. There were feminists – Code Pink – and busloads of hippie protesters who had arrived from Jordan. One night I came back to my hotel in Baghdad to find the Hollywood actor Sean Penn wandering around the lobby, looking lost.

We went to my room and smoked cigarettes. Penn wondered if there was any alcohol (Iraq was dry unless you smuggled in your own) and he talked about how he had come as an average citizen from Marin County, California, wanting to stop the war.

'It's up to the Iraqi people to get rid of their own leader,' he said, which was basically what everyone else, except the American military planners and George W. Bush, was saying too.

In a kind of fever in those last days of peacetime, I collected as many names and phone numbers of ordinary Iraqis as I could, as a wilful verification process. I wanted to go back after the war and find out how many of those people still lived, or how their lives had radically changed.

I went to monasteries, universities, libraries, archaeological sites and hospitals. I listened to the biblical stories of Jonah, who wandered northern Iraq, and the whale; of Assyrian kings; and of Nineveh, city of great sin. I traced maps of Mesopotamia, the ancient land that also included parts of what are now Kuwait, Syria and Turkey.

We stopped driving when it got dark, and slept in eerie, empty, chilly hotels where the Mukhabarat sat in the lobby with their cheap, cracked leather jackets and their drooping moustaches.

They were so horribly obvious, those spies. Don't they even bother to try to be discreet? I often asked Reem, but she shrugged and said that Iraqis had become so accustomed to them that they often forgot they were there. Still, for years afterwards – and even today when I return to Baghdad – I lower my voice when a waiter approaches a table and feel suspicious of all hotel staff.

In Baghdad hotels, the maids used to go through all our pockets, open our notebooks and search our drawers. There were rumours of secret cameras in our rooms to document indiscretions, which could be used later for extortion. I used to dress in my darkened bathroom and always talked to people with the television blaring, erasing the sound of our voices.

One sunny morning in Baghdad, Munzer and I talked our way into the Iraq Museum, pre-looting. Another time he got us into an obscure Baghdad museum devoted to gifts and tributes to Saddam: a testament to his egomania, like the towering statues and portraits of him everywhere.

But what I remember best in the haze of memory was going to the place that had come to be known as the mythical Hanging Gardens of Babylon. Reem and I spent a gloomy day wandering through the 'gardens', which were dishevelled and in disarray – a sad fate for one of the Seven Wonders of the World, if in fact they really did exist and were not just a poetic creation.

There were no green meadows arranged by Nebuchadnezzar for his queen, Amytis, and there was no Tower of Babel in the background. It was empty except for a lone family wandering through the ruins and a darkened gift shop selling key chains.

Saddam often compared himself to Nebuchadnezzar, the Chaldean king. Everyone knows how that story ended: he conquered Jerusalem and destroyed the temple. But according to the Book of Daniel in the Old Testament, Nebuchadnezzar was also humbled by God for his arrogance. The king went mad, succumbing to bouts of shrieking insanity and living in the wild for seven years.

Reem was often silent on these trips, sitting in the back seat with her oversized black plastic handbag at her feet. The Gardens of Babylon disturbed her: they seemed symbolic of fallen empires and worlds disappearing.

I knew she felt waves of endless anxiety about what lay ahead for her, her family and her country. Her studies had been halted, as had any plans for marriage. 'There's no future for anyone right now,' she said, with no hint of self-pity.

She stared out of the car window, taking in the endless rows of swaying date trees along the highway. Ali had told me once that the trees represented the soul of the Iraqis: their profound connection to their country, their sacred land and their identity. Those dreamy, plentiful trees haunted me after the invasion. The Iraqi soul had been lost.

The people we visited in those strange, dark days were mostly in a panic. The worshippers in the church in Mosul sat in the cold pews in tears, begging God to spare them from another war. They prayed in Aramaic, the language of Christ, which I found beautiful.

Shortly before Christmas 2002, the relics of St Teresa of Lisieux, a French saint known as 'the little flower of Jesus' who had died aged twenty-four from tuberculosis in 1897, arrived in Mosul. Then, there were nearly one million Christians in Iraq. Today, the figure is estimated to be as low as 200,000.

I sat with an older woman, blue-eyed and fair-skinned, bent over her rosary beads as the box of relics was carried through the church. She reminded me of my mother in her devotion and her courage.

She said she would not flee Iraq when the war started. 'Where will we go?' she whispered. 'The archbishop has begged the Christians not to leave. This is our home, our ancient land. If we go, we are deserting what is also ours.'

Together, we joined the snaking line that led to St Teresa's relics. As we approached, people bent in reverence to kiss the glass that shielded the bones as if the dead saint were a kind of talisman and protection from something dark ahead. Some people simply laid their cold palms on the glass beseechingly, looking inside.

The more I talked to people, the more I realised most of them had no plan for when 'zero hour' – the American invasion – actually came. No one really believes that a war is coming to one's doorstep. There was a sense of denial, a vague hope that someone – some diplomat, some world leader, or God – would stop it. I, on the other hand, had gone into panic mode and had four different locations in Baghdad where I stashed photocopies of my passport, water, food, batteries and boxes of Ciproflox, the antibiotic, in case of biological warfare – not that it would do much good.

It was in Mosul I realised, while talking to a Christian family who had begun some simple preparations – storing water in their cupboards and hoarding candles – that all of these ancient people were in grave danger of disappearing, as people so often did in Iraq: swallowed up like Jonah inside the whale, vanished.

In Bashiqa, a village not far from Mosul, we spent several days with the Yazidis, attending a wedding and a funeral. We stayed with a family and ate with the local mayor. The women remained in the kitchen, preparing vast dishes of incense-scented rice, and passing their fat babies back and forth. Aside from a few rusted Chevrolets parked outside their simple homes, the Yazidis' traditions had changed relatively little in the past two centuries.

One of the elders sat on the floor and explained their faith; he talked of how they were often wrongly accused of being devil worshippers, and of the injustices they suffered because of it. In fact, he said, they worshipped Lucifer, the Peacock God, the fallen angel. Their bible was something called the Black Book.

There was something simple and humble about the Yazidis'

dignity and isolation, and the fact that they were great survivors. They had been gravely persecuted through the ages, but most of all by Saddam.

Twelve years later, in the summer of 2014, the Islamic State (Isis) was racing through Iraq, swallowing up entire Yazidi and Christian villages, engulfing anyone who did not embrace its strict Salafist ways. The Yazidis were once again driven out, seeking refuge on a mountain near Sinjar, facing scorching temperatures by day and a lack of water, food and medical care. They were eventually rescued and brought to refugee camps, but Isis – at the time of this writing – controls most of the areas where they used to live. The Yazidis have become refugees and wanderers, as they feared.

A few days after Isis gained control of Mosul, raiding the Central Bank, driving out families and destroying all religious idolatry and statues of poets, I lay on my bed in my hotel in Baghdad, trying to organise my memories in the way that Iraqis do when they are talking about the past.

My Iraqi friends always refer to epochs: this was back in the Saddam days; that was when I fought in the Iran–Iraq War; this was during the first Gulf War; this was the second invasion; this was after the Americans came.

Iraq had been such a huge part of my life, but in 2004 I had a much-wanted child. After that, I returned to Iraq sporadically, but no longer lived there for months and months in bleak hotels.

There were to be no more sweeping drives through the countryside. Instead, there were requests to get inside the Green (or International) Zone to talk to the American occupiers. Mosul was no more; the ruins I had wandered through near the ancient city of Nineveh were held by Isis. There was no chance to even drive out of Baghdad.

But although I had returned from a long period away, I felt I had never really left Iraq, and clearly, it never really left me.

2

About nine months after the fall of Saddam, I lay in an isolation ward in a public hospital in a grey suburb south of Paris. It seemed there was a little piece of Iraqi earth inside me that refused to let me go.

It was January, and bitterly cold, and I was the only patient in the quarantine section. It was grim: long putty-coloured hallways where the lights flickered on and off; paper sheets on the cold hospital bed; a blinking television with four channels.

I was hooked into so many wires and tubes and needles that I could not move. My room truly was in isolation: I was so remotely placed that the nurses did not stop by often. I was also heavily pregnant. It seemed that my wish in Karbala with Reem had partially come true.

The unlucky part was that I was very ill. It seems – and no one knew for sure – I had contracted some kind of unique malady, and the doctors were pointing a finger at my time in Iraq. Dust from Iraq had found its way into my lungs; some kind of Iraqi virus had entered my body and stubbornly remained, embedded in tissues and floating freely in my bloodstream.

The doctors asked endless questions, most of which I could not answer: Had I been exposed to any chemical or biological weapons? (This was still in the days when George W. Bush and Tony Blair's lies about Saddam's weapons of destruction were not yet fully exposed.) Had I lived with a family, and drunk local water? Did it taste metallic? Had I been exposed to any nuclear waste? I thought I had, during a Ministry of Information-sponsored 'field trip' to Salman Pak, one of Saddam's key biological and chemical warfare centres.

In the end, medical science failed, the questions were never answered, and the doctors could not diagnose the illness, only treat the symptoms. I stayed in the isolation ward for several weeks, hooked up to a drip of some sort, bored and angry.

One day I woke at dawn, utterly confused about where I was,

and hauled myself out of bed. I dragged my IV pole behind me to a window in the hallway, and watched the snowfall line the hospital courtyard.

Back in my room, I turned on the TV and saw a video of a grizzled Saddam Hussein. A few weeks earlier he had been pulled from his hiding place – 'like a rat', as George W. Bush put it – a spider hole near Tikrit, where Reem and I had once watched proud Nebuchadnezzar-style military parades.

'Ladies and Gentlemen – we got him,' a jubilant Paul Bremer, the man appointed by the Americans to run Iraq, announced at a press conference later that day. But it was no triumph. I was no fan of Saddam's, but I sensed that a gigantic scab had been picked, leaving a raw and bleeding wound with no chance to heal.

Everyone had left Baghdad. Reem was in Dubai, Ali had gone into hiding and Munzer had run away. The country was being ripped apart at the seams: Munzer's prediction – 'We will fight!' – was correct. Everyone was fighting. The Sunni insurgents had risen up and were battling the US-led coalition; later they would go after local collaborators who worked with the new Iraqi security forces.

The doctors let me go home, eventually. When I signed the release forms, I felt that there were no answers to anything, and that sometimes things were meant to be shadowy, secretive and unknown.

I went back to Iraq when my baby son was six months old. My strange virus was gone, and my son was fat and cheerful. But by then, Iraq was another country: in the first stages of grieving, and loss.

3

On another trip, in 2011, I stayed with the writer Tamara Chalabi, whose father, Ahmed, had been the deputy prime minister of Iraq from 2005 to 2006, and one of the leading architects of the plan to topple Saddam Hussein.

The Chalabis are an old, wealthy and gracious Baghdadi family. Tamara is a historian educated at Harvard, who did her PhD on Shias in Lebanon, where her mother comes from. She was writing a memoir, the story of her father's political family, with recollections of a haughty and beautiful grandmother, grand palaces, lost Ottoman traditions. She was also involved in other projects to bring Baghdad some semblance of normality: trying to work with archivists at the National Library, establishing a young historians' prize and restoring the Chalabi farm near Kadhimiya.

The farm was an organic project intended to be adaptable so that people anywhere could benefit from good produce, which would save money and improve their health. But Tamara wanted first to try to 'purify' the soil, the earth that had been so badly 'traumatised'. It had been, she said, so damaged by the pain and sadness and the loss that had been bestowed on the country.

Tamara was training local women to plant and sow, and to use donkey manure and leaves as compost, and I watched them work under the blistering sun. The American troops were pulling out soon, and people were wondering how life would be after they were gone. One afternoon Tamara and I drove to the grave of Gertrude Bell, the British Arabist who had helped draw the map of modern Iraq in the wake of the break-up of the Ottoman Empire. All through my time living in Baghdad during the Saddam days I had been intrigued by Bell's life.

It was a tragic life. She had been deeply in love with two men, both statesmen as strong and vibrant as her. One was deemed unsuitable for marriage by her Victorian father's standards, and the other was already married and unable to leave his wife for Bell. The former died in Persia, the latter fighting in Gallipoli, and so deep was Bell's heartbreak that she took to the desert on horseback and began surveying and studying Arab tribes, seeking solace in her work. Her studies and map-making were brilliant, but her private life empty. She died, not yet sixty years old, by her own hand, in her Baghdad home. She was rumoured to have died a virgin. But she was nonetheless a brave, strong and inspirational woman who had loved Iraq with the kind of passion reserved for a first love.

During the Saddam days, I had often crept through a barbed-wire fence to visit the old uninhabited British Embassy on the river, where Bell and her rival and friend Freya Stark used to stay in between long desert trips. I would sit on the riverbank and imagine the parties that went on inside it in the time before Saddam – the whispers, the diplomatic intrigue, the swish of Bell's stiff silk evening gowns and the sight of her with a velvet ribbon around her neck, dressed for dinner after a day map-making.

For many years during the Saddam era, Bell's grave had been untended, and Tamara had started a project to restore it. As Tamara and I, in our headscarves and long abayas covering our bodies, bent in the hot sun to pull weeds, I wondered what Bell would think now of the hollow city and the destroyed country she'd loved so much.

Tamara's armed guards hovered near us as we stood looking at the grave. We drove to the farm silently in an armoured car. Everyone was worried about being stalled in traffic, and being a target for a car bomb.

4

I came back in 2014. Tamara's organic food project was on hold, as most things were. The American troops had pulled out two years earlier. The roads – aside from the ones in the International Zone where the embassies and United Nations were now located, utterly removed from the Iraqi population – were appallingly bad.

There seemed to be no easing up of the sorrow that had dogged the Iraqi people since the invasion. The city was expensive for my Iraqi friends, and car bombs were exploding again – there was one on the airport road the day before I arrived – and Isis was swallowing up entire swathes of countryside, farms, villages.

On 10 June, Isis drove into Mosul and raised their black flag. Then they moved to Tikrit, eventually getting stuck thirty kilometres from Baghdad, south of Samarra. They confiscated farm animals, grain supplies, oil, women and antiquities. They kidnapped anyone they thought would bring them cash. Women were ordered to put on headscarves. Christians fled. Isis wants a return to Islam in its strictest seventh-century form, as they believe it was practised by the prophet Muhammad. Anything else is not tolerated. If you are caught smoking, you are beaten and fined. A female dentist was beheaded for treating male patients. Bodies were found floating in the Tigris.

They took Raqqa, in Syria, as their capital, and installed strict sharia law. They started beheading Western hostages, including two of my journalist colleagues, Steven Sotloff and Jim Foley. And they kept fighting to take Iraq.

Soon there were reports that they were closer, in the Baghdad belt that surrounds the city. The fear was that while Isis was not poised to take the entire city, they could infiltrate it with sleeper cells and cause havoc with more car and roadside bombs.

It was heartbreaking to see the tension in the city after the fall of Mosul. These people who had lived through so much in the aftermath of the American invasion – sectarian killing sprees, roadside bombs that left headless corpses on the side of the road – were terrified once again.

Most of the Iraqis I had hired in my old office back in the Saddam days were gone. Omar, the second driver, was still around, but was rightly jittery. He made me wear an ugly head-to-toe polyester abaya that scratched my skin, and a brown scarf on my head wherever we went. He got twitchy when we were stuck in traffic.

He had a reason. His brother Yasser had been killed in a car bomb in 2010, leaving behind two small girls. He was only forty years old when he died. Wrong place, wrong time, but entire lives had been disassembled because of that explosive.

Badr, another interpreter, had recently moved to Maine with his second wife and his young family. His first wife had died because she could not get the proper treatment for a chronic liver disease in a Baghdad hospital, leaving Badr with a toddler. He wrote to me occasionally on Facebook, with wistful memories but also with foreboding prophecies of what would happen in the country he had left behind. He was homesick, but grateful to be gone. He feared that Iraq would be swallowed up by Isis, like a mouse swallowed up by a snake.

All of my Iraqi friends were trying to make new lives, but they were a mournful, sorrowful bunch. Whenever I met exiled Iraqis, in cafes in Paris or London or New York, they would speak about their country in the past tense. Nearly all of them had some story of horror, of family members being kidnapped or killed post-invasion. Isis seemed like another inevitable stage in this never-ending war, the eternal agony of Iraq.

Now the Shias, who had led the government since the American invasion, were going after ordinary Sunnis, under the guise of protecting themselves against Isis. There was the bitter memory of what they had suffered all those years when the Sunnis – the minority in Iraq – were in control. Now they had the power, and they were using it.

The militias on the streets were backed by Iran, the Shia giant in the region, who wanted to get a foothold in Iraq now that the chaos had started. Iraq was, once again, a republic of fear.

On a hazy summer morning in late June 2014, Omar drove me and another reporter to the Baghdad morgue.

Earlier I had spoken to a colleague, Duncan Spinner, who works for the International Commission on Missing Persons (ICMP), which matches bones in mass graves to missing people.

I had worked closely with ICMP in Bosnia, unearthing the remains of the dead from the genocide at Srebrenica. With the fall of Mosul, Spinner was in a dark mood. He was also worried about the Shia turning on the Sunni, and said that dozens of Sunni men had turned up in the morgue, including three boys from the same family.

During the gruesome years of the sectarian killings, which peaked in 2005–7, there were sometimes a hundred bodies a day brought into the morgue.

Spinner said it was not the number that defined a genocide, but the intent. 'The first step in genocide is a cycle of violence,' he said. 'You say something bad about people. Then you have blood on your hands.' He was worried that the death squads were back.

Inside, the morgue stank of rotting flesh. The doctor took us into a small office and showed us photographs of the dead. He said that all the Sunni men who had been brought in in the last few days showed signs of being tortured.

Down the hallway from where we talked, in a section of the building used by the Ministry of Interior, a prisoner was being held, blindfolded, bent over like a bird. When I asked the doctor why he was being held, he waved a hand. 'Forget it. Detainee.' I never found out what his crime was, or why the Ministry of Interior was holding him.

Families searching for their loved ones at the morgue sat in a small room with a television screen above them. One woman called Sammaya had come to look for her brother, Saleh, who had disappeared several days before.

Photographs of bullet-riddled corpses came up on the screen above her head; finally, Sammaya recognised one bloated, purple-bruised body: Saleh.

When she saw his familiar blue T-shirt, Sammaya put her hand over her mouth and began to sob, rocking back and forth. Saleh was a Sunni, and she said the Shia militias had come for him. She was not sure why – he was a teacher, and she knew he was not involved in any radical Sunni activities.

He ran to hide in a cupboard when they came, but they found him and dragged him off. They took him away, and that was the last Sammaya saw of him, until she saw him dead.

The screen showed photographs of a butcher and his son. Both were covered in blood.

'The son got a head shot, probably a chest shot too,' the pathologist said. 'The father –' He looked closer at the screen and confirmed. 'Head shot.'

'Militias?'

The pathologist shrugged. 'Who knows? Who else?'

He shifted the image to another dead body.

'Shia against Sunni, Sunni against Shia, what does it all mean? We are all Arabs,' he said emphatically. 'This is just revenge of the idiots.'

5

Baghdad in late November was less tense than in June, when Isis was at the doorstep of the capital and there were plans to evacuate the embassies. A new government under a more inclusive prime minister, Haider al-Abadi, a Shia, had been installed. He was attempting to both root out corruption in the Iraqi Army and rein in the chaos.

But it was far from calm. The American air strikes had begun in the autumn, and yet Isis was still operating with impunity, killing, raping and stealing. It was said to be making a million dollars a day by trading looted oil with its mortal enemies – Syria and Kurdistan – as well as kidnapping and claiming hostage fees, stealing antiquities, overturning profitable farms and silos of grain. Its leaders also imposed fines on Christians and anyone that did not follow their laws – if they did not kill them.

Everyone feared Isis and saw it as an existential threat, but people were also beginning to square off into real sectarian divides.

Neighbourhoods were divided into recruitment centres for Shia militias who were trained to fill in the gap the inept Iraqi Army had left, then sent out to the so-called belt of Baghdad to fight against Isis. I stopped to talk to some of the young fighters who had just come back from the front lines in Amerli, and in Kirkuk. They had joined up willingly, answering a 'fatwa' to arms by their highest spiritual leader, the Ayatollah Ali al-Sistani.

But what were these young Shias' goals for the future? Did they want a Shia fiefdom? Could they ever live with Sunnis again after Isis? Were there any moderates left, on either side?

In an embarrassing U-turn for President Obama, American troops came back in small numbers after they had been pulled out. American special military advisers were talking to Sunni tribal leaders in Anbar, and peshmerga fighters in Kurdistan, in the hope of enlisting them as moderate Sunnis in the fight against Isis.

'It's a mess,' Omar said one morning as we had a vanilla-scented coffee in a cafe on the banks of the Tigris. 'The dark days are coming back.'

From the corner of my eye, I saw a large man with dyed red hair. I stared at him, and he stared back. I realised, with a shock, that it was one of my former nemeses from the Saddam days, an informant from the Ministry of Information. He was one of the men I had had to go to, to beg to stay in the country. To get a new visa, one had to pay – with money, or with goods. Once, I saw a reporter bribe the red-headed man and his colleague with a live goat to be slaughtered for Eid.

'Don't talk to him!' Omar hissed. 'Remember how bad he was? Remember how difficult he made your life?'

The bad man had put on weight, lots of it, since the Saddam years, and he looked much older. I wondered what had happened to him in the dozen years since the chaos began, but in a sense I did not really want to know.

The day before I left, in al-Mansour, a Baghdad neighbourhood, I had tea with a professor of English, a translator of Faulkner, Fitzgerald, Hemingway and Shakespeare. Dr Sadek Mohammed had come back to Iraq after a long period of exile in India. When he arrived home in 2007, he found the Baghdad he had left behind unrecognisable.

'The electricity was out, garbage filling the streets, people changing entirely before my eyes,' he said. 'I could see the writing on the wall. We had lost Baghdad forever. This wasn't my city! This wasn't my city!' He spoke with the air of a man beyond anguish.

Sadek showed me a poem he had written in this period of 'disbelief' at what had happened to his country.

> Three Scenes, One City
> Baghdad 2007
>
> I
>
> Thick forests of cold cement
> their trees are planted
> by veiled creatures that look like men
> and masters of falsehood, flattery and madness.
> Flowers didn't bloom this spring.
>
> II
>
> Demons have their wily rhythms.
> They plant bombs
> behind every stone
> and check our stealthy motion
> in offices, markets and classrooms.
>
> III
>
> Poems are engulfed in darkness
> and what's in the street is dull and sullen.
> The poet's heart leans on the solitary lamp post
> and his eyes gaze at his famished children.

When I asked him to identify the losses sustained by the city, by the country, he paused.

'The greatest loss was that the Americans did not have a plan,' he said simply. 'And so, I could sit here and give you all the losses one by one. I could tell you about the careless American soldiers writing graffiti on the lions at Babylon; the archaeological sites that have been looted; our cultural history gone. I could tell you about our writers being isolated here – and Iraq is the place where the first writing was developed!

'But really, what we have lost is that we once did feel united. We do not any more. What is Iraq? Who is an Iraqi?'

Sadek said this was his greatest fear: more than the car bombs, more than the winter approaching and the lack of money in the country, which equals lack of freedom, more even than Isis. 'The biggest fear,' he said, 'is that if we lose our sense of unity – Iraq will be lost forever.' ∎

OBSERVATOIRES

Noémie Goudal

I n her series *Observatoires,* Noémie Goudal places stairs, pyramids
and domes in natural, isolated, timeless spaces.

The structures were originally photographed in Germany, the
United Kingdom and France. The images were then printed on
paper, which were stuck on card to form cut-outs. Finally, Goudal
restages and reshoots these cardboard templates.

In their new setting, these two-dimensional paper structures take
on an ephemeral quality. The folds in the cut-outs are left deliberately
discernible, highlighting their fleeting existence in photographic
space and their rough-and-ready construction.

Isolated and incongruous, the man-made structures and their
seemingly conflicting settings play on our sense of scale, on what
is natural, what is artifice, what belongs. Inspired by the cosmic
architecture of India such as the observatories of Jai Singh II,
Goudal's *Observatoires* are likewise orientated towards the sky,
observing it relentlessly. ■

1. *Observatoire IX*

2. *Observatoire V*

3. *Observatoire X*

4. *Observatoire VII*

5. *Observatoire III*

6. *Observatoire IV*

7. Observatoire VI

More ways
to read *Granta*

Subscribers can now read everything from this issue
and access *Granta*'s entire digital archive
on our brand new website.

Print subscription $48
New! Includes digital access

Digital subscription $17
Special launch price

Call 845 267 3031, complete the subscription
form overleaf or visit granta.com

© MARK DORF

GRANTA

THE MAGAZINE OF NEW WRITING

PRINT SUBSCRIPTION REPLY FORM FOR US, CANADA AND LATIN AMERICA
(includes digital access). For digital-only subscriptions, please visit granta.com.

GUARANTEE: If I am ever dissatisfied with my *Granta* subscription, I will simply notify you, and you will send me a complete refund or credit my credit card, as applicable, for all un-mailed issues.

YOUR DETAILS

TITLE ....

NAME ....

ADDRESS ....

....

CITY.. STATE ....

ZIP CODE .... COUNTRY................................

EMAIL ....

☐ Please check this box if you do not wish to receive special offers from *Granta*

☐ Please check this box if you do not wish to receive offers from organizations
    selected by *Granta*

YOUR PAYMENT DETAILS

1 year subscription: ☐ US: $48 ☐ Canada: $56 ☐ Latin America: $68

3 year subscription: ☐ US: $120 ☐ Canada: $144 ☐ Latin America: $180

Enclosed is my check for $ _____ made payable to *Granta*.

Please charge my: ☐ Visa ☐ MasterCard ☐ Amex

Card No. ☐☐☐☐☐☐☐☐☐☐☐☐☐☐☐☐

Expiration date ☐☐ / ☐☐

Security Code ☐☐☐☐

SIGNATURE .... DATE ....

Please mail this order form with your payment instructions to:

Granta Publications
PO Box 359
Congers, NY 10920-0359

Or call 845-267-3031
Or visit GRANTA.COM for details

Source code: BUS131PM

'It is a matter of time before we get you, worshippers of the cross.'
Graffiti on church building, Kessab, 2014
Courtesy of the author

THE BATTLE FOR KESSAB

Charles Glass

G aro Manjikian is a strongly built farmer with a degree in chemistry and a flourishing moustache like those in sepia photographs of Armenian gentlemen from the late Ottoman era. On the evening of 20 March last year, he was having dinner at George's Restaurant in the woods where Syria's Mediterranean shore adjoins Turkey's. At his restaurant table, he told me, were five of his friends and their families. Their discussion turned to the conflict, entering its fourth year, to unseat Syrian president Bashar al-Assad. 'The mayor of Kessab was with us. We asked him about the situation,' Manjikian recalled. 'He was very quiet.'

Kessab is the only Armenian town in Syria, although other Syrian villages and cities have Armenian minorities. Perched on a hillside within sight of the Turkish frontier, its 2,000-plus inhabitants also include about five hundred Alawite Muslims and Arab Christians. In the summer, tens of thousands of tourists used to fill its hotels and guest houses to bursting. The beaches, pine forests and fruit orchards hosted camps for Armenian Boy Scouts, as well as hikers, picnickers and Saudis seeking respite from stifling desert heat. In addition to the three churches for the Armenian Orthodox, Catholic and Protestant congregations, a large, modern mosque occupies a prominent position.

The conflict was killing tourism in Kessab. Incomes were down, hotels empty. Family visits to Aleppo, with its large Armenian population, became impossible after rebels occupied parts of the city in July 2012. Yet until now the conflict had left the region relatively unscathed. The greatest calamity to hit the town in 2013, apart from the decline in tourism, was not the war between al-Assad's supporters and opponents but unseasonal hailstorms that destroyed the peach and apple crops.

However, events elsewhere in Syria were conspiring to engulf Kessab. On 16 March 2014, the Syrian Army with its Hezbollah allies expelled opposition forces from the town of Yabroud near the Lebanese border. This cut the opposition's supply line from Lebanon and left the government dominant in most of western Syria. When the rebel leadership organised a response to threaten the regime's coastal bastion of Latakia, their line of march led directly through Kessab.

Throughout March, one portent after another had made the Armenians of north-west Syria apprehensive. First, smugglers tipped off inhabitants that militant jihadists were gathering nearby in parts of south-west Turkey that had not seen them before. Then, Syrian farmers living beside the international frontier noticed gunmen mustering on the Turkish side.

By 18 March, regular Turkish Army units were disappearing from the forts guarding the twenty-five-mile border between Turkish Hatay and Syrian Kessab. Bearded paramilitaries in assorted non-Turkish uniforms were replacing them. A United Nations source confirmed what Manjikian told me. 'Large numbers of fighters in minivans were going up the mountain. A Turkish Army convoy was coming down.' The UN and the Syrian military received reports on 19 March that guerrillas in Turkey were moving dangerously close to Kessab. It seemed that the Turkish Army was relinquishing control of the border to ragged units of the Syrian opposition, although no one in Syria knew why.

On 20 March, while Garo Manjikian and Kessab's Mayor Vazgen Chaparyan discussed politics over spicy sujuk sausages and Syrian wine, a fellow Armenian from Kessab telephoned the Syrian Army's central command thirty miles to the south in Latakia. He relayed widespread fears of imminent rebel infiltration from Turkey. The commander dismissed the man's worries on the grounds that an old agreement making the Turkish Army responsible for security north and east of Kessab was still in force. The Armenians were not reassured.

At four o'clock the next morning, 21 March, residents of the village of Gözlekçiler in Turkey observed paramilitary units driving through border checkpoints towards Kessab. They later told the *Economist*'s veteran Turkey correspondent, Amberin Zaman, that the Turkish military had evacuated civilians from Gözlekçiler and prohibited journalists from entering the area.

A half-hour later in Kessab, an artillery bombardment woke the Catholic pastor of St Michael the Archangel Church, Father Nareg Louisian. 'The sounds became louder. The Turkish Army attacked our village,' the 43-year-old priest told me. 'Everybody felt it was a dangerous situation. We ran away. At the beginning, we thought it would be for some hours and it will finish.'

Residents of Sakhra, one of a dozen scattered hamlets and villages near Kessab, watched guerrilla fighters massing over the border in Turkey. They summoned Syrian border police. 'The rebels shot at them at 5.30,' a United Nations official said. 'The Syrian border police shot back.' Minutes later, assisted by mortar fire from Turkey, other rebels assaulted the Syrian police post at Qommeh. The battle for Kessab had begun.

Garo Manjikian woke as usual at 5.30 a.m. to start work in his family's apple orchards between Kessab and Sakhra. 'I heard voices from the Syrian police station,' he told me when we met in Kessab six months later. 'Then I heard guns. Then, after half an hour, explosions. Missiles. At 6.30, I saw with my eyes the Sakhra police station.' By then, he recalled, it had become 'a column of fire'. He woke his father and mother. As he struggled to move his mother, who was dying of cancer, the telephone rang. An Arab Christian woman from Sakhra begged Manjikian for help. She worked at Latakia's university, where his children had studied. He drove to her house beside the border to rescue her, with her mother and son. Two mortars barely missed them, and he made it back home. Both families, including Manjikian's three children, crammed into his light pickup truck. 'There was not time to take my documents or my diploma,' he said. A barrage of mortar fire hastened their departure. It was nine o'clock when they reached the village of Nab'ain, about five miles south. 'When we saw the mortars hit Nab'ain, I knew this was going to be longer than we imagined.' They fled again, this time all the way down to Latakia.

That evening, Syrian television broadcast the arrival of most of Kessab's inhabitants at St Mary's Armenian Orthodox Church in Latakia. Many of the two thousand men, women and children who fled Kessab crowded into the nave, the adjoining school and the church hall. Some had not had time to put on their day clothes, and most lacked basic provisions.

In Damascus, Armenian scholar Dr Nora Arissian watched her compatriots on television. 'I saw them in their pyjamas,' she said, 'and it was 1915 again.'

No Armenian can forget 1915. From 24 April 1915, which Armenians commemorate as the beginning of a slaughter that in fact started earlier, the Ottoman Empire killed between 650,000 and 1.5 million Armenians in their homes, on death marches and in concentration camps. Some were murdered outright, while others died from starvation, disease, frost in the mountains or dehydration on the plain.

The genocide had historical roots. In the late nineteenth century, rebels in Bulgaria and Serbia, with Russian, British and French encouragement, massacred Muslims and caused the flight of hundreds of thousands of Muslim refugees to Turkish Anatolia. Turkish rulers, who had lost almost all their European lands in the Balkans, feared that leaving Christian, non-Turkish majorities in their eastern provinces would lead to further partition. That belief lay behind the removal of Armenians from areas where they predominated, while leaving small Armenian minorities elsewhere. Removal, however, meant murder. Talat Pasha, one of the triumvirate of Young Turks who ruled the empire from behind the sultan's throne during the First World War, told a German consul in June 1915: 'What we are dealing with here . . . is the annihilation of the Armenians.'

When Turkey joined the German war against the Allies, in 1914, its leaders had dreams of expanding the empire through Russian territory to include the Turkish-speaking regions of Central Asia. Their attempt to invade the Russian Empire collapsed in January 1915, when the Russians smashed the advancing Turkish Third Army at Sarikamish in the mountains of eastern Turkey. Between 60,000 and 90,000 Ottoman soldiers died in battle or froze to death. Turkey's leaders blamed Armenians as the ostensible 'enemy within', although Armenian soldiers lay among the Ottoman dead. From then on, the Armenians were doomed. Armenian men between the ages of twenty and forty-five, all of whom had been conscripted into the army, were disarmed. Commanders forced them into labour battalions, digging trenches, paving roads and cutting trees. Those who did not die of overwork, disease and starvation were taken out in small groups and executed. Armenian women, children and elderly men were left without protectors. The Turks gave some of them a few days to sell their property, at a fraction of its value, and to pack their clothes. Others were driven from their houses in their pyjamas with no time to gather any possessions. Turkish police and troops deported the defenceless civilians on what were in effect death marches to the desert in Syria. En route to Deir Ezzor, more than two hundred miles through the desert from Aleppo, they were robbed, raped, kidnapped, starved and tortured.

The remnant who made it to the concentration camps were enslaved, butchered or burned to death. A few brave Turkish, Kurdish and Arab civilians provided refuge to Armenians, sometimes adopting the children in order to save them. Thousands of Armenian women were forced into marriage with Muslim men, while others suffered rape by soldiers or tribesmen.

Following the armistice between Turkey and the Allies on 30 October 1918, the killing stopped, leaving traumatised survivors, along with the Armenians of Istanbul and a few other large cities who were not deported. Some tried to go back to Turkish Armenia, but the Turks drove them out. A few hundred remained in the village of Vakifli on the Turkish side of the border north of Kessab, but most emigrated to the Americas or settled in Lebanon and Syria. A country called Armenia, the eastern portion of the ancient nation that had little connection to western Armenia of the Ottomans, rose out of the war as a socialist republic of the Soviet Union. Like Syria and Lebanon, it gave shelter to refugees from Turkey.

Many Turks and Kurds today have Armenian grandmothers, a fact some deny and others have come to embrace. One day, a Kurdish waiter at a riverside restaurant outside Damascus interrupted my conversation with Missak Baghboudarian, the musical director and chief conductor of Syria's National Symphony Orchestra, to ask Missak whether he was Armenian. When Missak responded in the affirmative, the waiter said that his grandmother was Armenian. He looked proud of the fact. When the waiter left, Missak compared the Kurds, who participated in the genocide, to the Turks: 'The Kurds admit they made a mistake. That is the difference.'

Dr Arissian is a young history professor at Damascus University whose gentle voice belies her determination to bring attention to the Armenian tragedy. I met with her during my visit to Syria in autumn 2014. 'The Syrian press was the first to use the word "genocide" about the Armenians, in 1917,' she told me over espresso at Il Caffè di Roma in Kassa'a, a Christian neighbourhood near Damascus's ancient walled city. She discovered during her research that Syrian Arabic newspapers like *Al Asima*, *Alef Baa* and *Al Muktabas* reported on the mass deportations of Armenians as they took place. Despite Ottoman censorship, the papers published stories with the terms 'extermination', 'annihilation', 'uprooting the race'. The Arabic word for genocide, she said, was *ibada*, which appeared often in the Syrian press during the First World War.

The immediacy with which Dr Arissian spoke of Armenian genocide was new. Most of the Armenians who spoke to me in Damascus before I drove up to Kessab last autumn talked about genocide, past and possibly future, when in years past their conversation had been about food, drink, love affairs and Mid-East politics. Something changed in March 2014 to make the only topic of conversation genocide, and fear of genocide.

Despite their apprehensions, most of them had no desire to leave Syria. Dr Arissian said, 'The Armenian genocide made the Armenians in Syria grateful to Syria.' In Syria, they had built churches, schools, social clubs, sports centres and businesses. There were no restrictions on speaking or publishing in Armenian. Armenians constituted a separate, respected community, whose honesty and industry were acknowledged by Syria's Arabs and Kurds. 'In Aleppo, any Arab who wants to repair his watch or his shoes goes to an Armenian,' she said. 'They know the Armenians are straight. You never find an Armenian thief.' True or not, this is the popular perception in Syria among Armenians and non-Armenians alike.

'Once, I did not do my homework,' Missak Baghboudarian recalled of his Damascus childhood. 'My teacher told me that, until now, we Armenians have a good reputation. You must keep that reputation.' Armenian leaders in the refugee shanty towns of the 1920s forbade criminal activity and prostitution that would shame their community. Memories of rape and forced marriages were strong. The refugees had neither property nor money, but they worked hard to create businesses and move out of the camps. In Damascus and Aleppo, they joined a middle-class community of Armenians who had lived in Syria since at least the sixteenth century. The communities melded and ensured their survival by staying out of politics.

Their acceptance in Syrian society became evident when the people of Kessab fled to Latakia in 2014. One Kessab Armenian told me, 'We must be proud to be Syrian, because all the ethnic mosaic of Latakia – the Alawis, the Sunnis and the Christians – helped us.' Dr Arissian believed that the war was bringing Armenians closer to their fellow Syrians. 'Before the war, I said we are not integrated in the Syrian community. But I was wrong.'

The temptation to emigrate, however, had always been strong, due to decades of instability, tyranny and intermittent threats from Islamic exclusivists seeking a pure Sunni Muslim Syria. In 1960, there were about 150,000 Armenians in Syria. The numbers steadily declined to 115,000 in 1996. Last August, Bishop Armash Nalbandian, the primate of the Armenian Orthodox Church in Damascus, told me that about 30,000 Syrian Armenians had left since the war began. 'Nobody has sold his property or his house,' he added. 'They are waiting to come back.' This may be optimistic, but Armenians who remain in Syria fear the fate of their more numerous brethren in Paris and Los Angeles: assimilation into Western culture leading to loss of language and faith. It is within Islamic Syria, paradoxically, that they feel most Armenian. 'We like Armenia,' Kessab farmer Garo Manjikian said, 'but we love Syria. This is my country. We can keep our originality here. We can keep our identity in this Muslim environment more than in the West.' Bishop Nalbandian, speaking in his office next to the Armenian school in Damascus, echoed Manjikian. 'We witnessed a new kind of Islam. We were persecuted in Turkey, because we were not Muslim. My grandparents came as refugees. We were welcomed.'

An Armenian house decorator named Samir Mikho told me over coffee in his modest flat in Dweila, a mixed Damascus neighbourhood of Muslims, Christian Arabs and Armenians, that Syria would always be his home. 'A century ago, my parents left their country,' he said. 'Their church became a stable. We don't want that to happen here.' Mikho's resolve to stay was unexpected in light of the fact that, a year earlier, a mortar shell hit the Armenian school's bus stop and killed his ten-year-old daughter, Vanessa.

This year, Armenians mark the centenary of the massacres. It may have been no more than a coincidence that German officers, whose empire was allied to the Ottomans, participated in some of the bloodletting. During the First World War, the Allies declared Turkey's deeds 'crimes against humanity', originating a term they would later apply to Nazi actions. British Prime Minister David Lloyd George called what befell the Armenians then a 'holocaust'. After 1945, Germany recognised its guilt and made some restitution. Turkey never did.

Now a new generation of Turkish historians, notably Taner Akçam in his epic *A Shameful Act: The Armenian Genocide and the Question of Turkish Responsibility*, has taken the risk of using the word, with its implications of moral culpability and the obligation to redress wrongs. The expulsions and murders of the Ottoman Empire's Armenian subjects continued until Turkey lost the war and the Allies occupied Istanbul. It resumed for a time under the nationalist government of Mustafa Kemal Atatürk. Atatürk himself later conceded that it was 'a shameful act', subsequently the title of Akçam's powerful book.

To this day, however, Turkey's official position is that the Armenians brought disaster on themselves by supporting the empire's enemies. The government has forbidden its citizens to utter the word 'genocide': Article 301 of the Turkish Penal Code makes it an offence to 'insult Turkishness', and those convicted can be sentenced to ten years in prison. Armenian writer Hrant Dink, who was assassinated in 2011, novelist Elif Shafak and Nobel Laureate Orhan Pamuk have all been prosecuted under Article 301.

Turkey's continuing denial made Armenians around the world particularly sensitive to the occupation of Kessab in 2014. It was as if modern Germany, while refusing to acknowledge its genocide of Jews, had unleashed bands of neo-Nazi skinheads on a Jewish town over the border with Holland. As Dutch Jews would discern a German hand in their victimisation, Armenians understandably saw Turkey's. Moreover, Kessab was a last corner of the medieval Armenian Kingdom of Cilicia that fell in 1375. The oldest Armenian church in the region, St Stephen's, built in the tenth century, is located there. Turkey had ethnically cleansed Kessab twice, during the pogroms of 1909, when it also killed 30,000 Armenians in Adana, and in 1915. Both times, the people returned and rebuilt. Thus the attack on Kessab resonated more with the Armenian diaspora than the rebel attacks on Armenian quarters in other Syrian towns.

The 2014 conquest of Kessab was not a repetition of 1915. There was no massacre, possibly because most of the inhabitants fled. The first casualty was 24-year-old Gevorg Juryan, whom, Catholic Father Louisian conceded, rebels might have mistaken for a soldier because he wore military-style boots. 'They left his body in front of his house,' he said. 'The family begged to be allowed to bury him, but they allowed it only after three days.' Fighting between army and rebels killed another Armenian civilian, but two deaths do not constitute genocide. The jihadists spared twenty or so aged villagers who were too infirm to escape. They were escorted to the border, and the Turkish Army drove them to the Armenian village in Turkey, Vakifli, about twenty-five miles north. Syria, which by then had suffered more than 150,000 deaths in its increasingly savage war, had witnessed far worse.

Yet the jihadists called their offensive in Kessab *al-Anfal*, 'the spoils', from a chapter in the Quran:

> And know that whatever ye take as spoils of war, lo! a
> fifth thereof is for Allah, and for the messenger and for
> the kinsman (who hath need) and orphans and the needy
> and the wayfarer, if ye believe in Allah . . .

Al-Anfal was a provocative term. The last military campaign to take the name *al-Anfal* was Saddam Hussein's 1988 slaughter of more than 100,000 Kurds in northern Iraq, belatedly condemned around the world as genocide. In 1915, the Ottoman state distributed the spoils seized from deported Armenians – land, houses, furniture, books, jewellery and clothing – to its Muslim subjects. In Kessab in 2014, similarly, the jihadists looted houses, churches, hotels and shops, trucking much of the booty to Turkey.

A minority of the rebels were from the American-supported Syrian National Coalition, but most belonged to Sunni fundamentalist factions, like the Islamic Front, Ansar ash-Sham and al-Qaeda's official wing in Syria, the Nusra Front. They transformed Kessab into a barracks, commandeering abandoned houses and hotels. They posted their destruction of church crucifixes on social media, but did little other damage in the first week.

A day later, rebels moved south to the region's highest summit, Observatory 45, where a television transmission tower overlooked most of Latakia Province. The hilltops changed hands several times, as the opposition and the Syrian Army fought bitter battles for the high ground. On 23 March, a Turkish warplane downed a Syrian jet attempting to bomb the Nusra Front rebels near Kessab, and Turkish Prime Minister Recep Tayyip Erdoğan praised the pilot. Meanwhile, opposition artillery exploded near the Armenians' refuge inside St Mary's Church in Latakia. They felt they had nowhere to hide from forces they viewed as nothing more than Turkey's mercenaries.

By the end of March 2014, rebels with Turkish air cover and artillery support controlled most of the Kessab region. On 1 April, the head of the Syrian National Coalition, Ahmad Asi Al-Jarba, came to Observatory 45 to be photographed with his men and their Islamist allies. Other rebels posted video pictures of themselves in the sea below George's Restaurant, where Garo Manjikian and Mayor Vazgen Chaparyan had dined the night before they fled. There were now two wars: one for territory, the other for public opinion.

Rival propaganda machines manufactured evidence for the Internet, television and the press. Accounts by jihadists, the Turkish government and media on the one hand and the Syrian government and media and overseas Armenian lobbies on the other conflicted in every detail. It became almost impossible, especially with no journalists able to enter Kessab without risking rebel kidnapping, to sift truth from fiction.

The Turkish press peddled an image of benevolent jihadists in Kessab. One article stated that two octogenarian sisters, Sirpuhi and Satenik Titizyan, were grateful to the fundamentalists for rescuing them and bringing them to 'paradise' in Turkey. However, in a subsequent interview with Istanbul's Armenian newspaper, *Agos*, the sisters said, 'The bearded men came to our home. They spoke Turkish. They rifled through our belongings and asked if we had guns.' The paper added, 'The two women reported that they were deported to the Turkish border, even though they told the men that they wanted to leave for the Syrian port city of Latakia.'

One Armenian paper, *Asbarez* of Los Angeles, claimed that Turks and rebels had murdered eighty Armenians in Kessab. Other overseas Armenians disseminated reports of mass killings and posted photos and videos that included the bloody corpse of a woman with a crucifix rammed into her mouth. It later transpired that the photo was from *Inner Depravity*, a 2005 Canadian horror film.

Armenians worldwide mobilised behind the #SaveKessab social-media campaign. Armenian-American television celebrity Kim Kardashian, whose public persona would previously have offended Syria's conservative Armenians, tweeted: 'Please let's not let history repeat itself!!!!!! Let's get this trending!!!! #SaveKessab #ArmenianGenocide.' Mayor Chaparyan tried to set the record straight, declaring, 'Armenians [have not been] killed. I do not know where these rumours are being created.'

Nonetheless, the Armenian disinformation campaign was having an effect. Four members of the US Congress wrote to President Barack Obama on 28 March: 'With the Christian Armenian community being uprooted from its homeland, yet again, we strongly urge you to take all necessary measures without delay to safeguard the Christian Armenian community of Kessab.' On 2 April, California Congressman Adam Schiff questioned American UN Ambassador Samantha Power, a vocal supporter of anti-Assad rebels, about Kessab's Armenians. Schiff stated that 'there is a particular poignancy to their being targeted in this manner'. One week later, six members of Congress denounced Turkey at a news conference in Washington. The Armenian National Committee urged the president and Congress to compel Turkey to cease its support for another genocide of Armenians. An online petition demanded that the US stop 'history repeating itself'. Despite the Armenian lobby's exaggerations and distortions, the onslaught was forcing Turkey to weigh its patronage of the rebels in Kessab against the harm to its relationship with the West.

On Tuesday, 3 June, Turkey for the first time branded the Nusra Front that had led the assault on Kessab a 'terrorist organisation'. Turkish support for al-Nusra and its allies gradually dried up in the Kessab region, easing the way for a Syrian Army offensive. Although Turkey continued to allow jihadists to enter Syria along the rest of the five-hundred-mile border, Kessab became a no-go area for the jihadis. Syrian government forces took the town on 15 June, ending a three-month occupation. The people began returning the next day.

Garo Manjikian told me that he returned within hours of Kessab's liberation. He reopened his grocery store, but his tractors and other farm equipment had been stolen. He and some friends founded the Syrian Armenian Committee for Urgent Relief and Rehabilitation of Kessab to oversee reconstruction. Strangely, I did not see Syrian soldiers in the town. Apart from a few checkpoints on the roads outside, there was no military presence to defend the area from a second rebel invasion. And there was little if any fear of it. 'The Turks will not do the same thing again,' Manjikian said with confidence, placing his trust in the Armenian lobby in the US.

Although the rebels damaged the town, they did not destroy it. Most buildings were intact, but windows were smashed, doors removed and furniture looted. The rebels were not alone in the pillaging – one house that I visited had been looted by 'liberators' from the Syrian Army. The jihadist occupiers took a special interest in pianos, destroying every single one. The Armenian Cultural Centre's

CHARLES GLASS

music school had been teaching piano to twenty-seven students. The Cultural Centre had been burned, along with its books and pictures.

The pastors of the three Christian denominations took me on a tour of their churches. They were pleased that so many members of their respective flocks had returned, although about 20 per cent stayed in Latakia or left Syria. 'We cannot stop people emigrating,' Pastor Sevag Trashian said, 'but the majority of our community wants to stay here. We want to return Kessab to its good days. We have our own contribution as Christians and as Armenians to this mosaic.'

The three clerics showed me the damage to their churches, the desecration, the burned books, the slashed paintings. Artisans labouring to restore the church buildings had yet to remove the jihadists' Arabic graffiti:

> Soldiers of the Only One were here. God willing, we will crush the Christians, Armenians and Alawis.

> We will go after you wherever you go, God willing.

> Do not rejoice, Christians. We will step on you.

> It is a matter of time before we get you, worshippers of the cross.

In Deir Ezzor, where a century ago thousands of Armenians had been herded into camps, starved and killed, jihadis blew up the Armenian Genocide Memorial Church. They then scattered the bones of the victims who perished between 1915 and 1918.

The first time I visited Kessab was in 1987. My friend Armen Mazloumian, whose grandfather founded the famous Baron's Hotel in Aleppo, escorted me to the Evangelical Protestant church. It was as austere as any Presbyterian kirk in Scotland, devoid of Eastern Christianity's icons, incense and statues. The only decoration was a childlike painting that I described at the time:

1

It showed Jesus Christ, the Good Shepherd, holding in His arms the body of a slain boy, the boy's head and arms dangling like Christ's own in Michelangelo's *Pietà*. Behind Him were the mountains of Armenia, and at His feet was a mound of skulls and bones with the date '1915' written on them. The caption was in Armenian, which Armen translated: 'So much blood. Let our grandchildren forgive you.'

The painting, like everything else in all of Kessab's churches, had been burned. ∎

Release the Darkness to New Lichen

but I found a way to say no
to the wood in my house

it kept creaking
wouldn't stop talking

I found a way to say no

I need to be standing
in the warmth of the wood
that the sun made

I need to find myself dissolving

otherwise it is all otherwise
I'm lost, did I say that

I saw the frill of light today
walking on the path

could you hear the stirring
in the wood, pine needles
and the branches

was it wind or a creature
am I here or is it over

this was the first day
the nothing day
in the nothing year

it gave me courage

it gave hints of blue,
clouds, electric
and dancing

it gave me rays
I've never seen

shooting down
touching things

this was the first day

NOTHING EVER HAPPENS HERE

Ottessa Moshfegh

The house was white stucco, ranch-style, with tall hedges and a large semicircular driveway. There was a crumbling pool out back full of rust stains and carcasses of squirrels that had fallen in and slowly starved to death. I used to tan out there on a lawn chair before auditions, fantasizing about getting rich and famous. My room had green shag carpeting and a twin-size bed on a plywood frame, a little nightstand with a child's lamp in the shape of a clown. Above my bed hung an old framed poster of Marlon Brando in *One-Eyed Jacks*. It would have done me well if I'd prayed to that poster, but I'd never even heard of Marlon Brando before. I was eighteen. I was living in an area of Los Angeles called Hancock Park: manicured lawns, big clean houses, expensive cars, a country club. Walking around those quiet streets, I felt like I was on the set of a soap opera about the private lives of business executives and their sexy wives. One day I'd star in something like that, I hoped. I had limited experience as an actor in high school, first as George in *Our Town* and then as Romeo in *Romeo and Juliet*. People had told me I looked like a sandy-haired Pierce Brosnan. I was broke, and I was a nobody, but I was happy.

Those first few months in Los Angeles, I lived off powdered cinnamon doughnuts and orange soda, fries from Astro Burger, and occasional joints rolled with stale weed my stepdad had given me back in Utah as a graduation present. Most days I took the bus around Hollywood, listening to the Eagles on my Walkman and imagining what life was like for all those people way up in the hills. I'd walk up Rossmore, which turned into Vine once you hit Hollywood, and then I'd get on a crosstown local down Santa Monica Boulevard. I liked to sit with all the young kids in school uniforms, the teenage runaways in rags and leather jackets, the crazies, the drunks, housekeepers with their romance novels, old men with their spittle, whores with their hairspray. This was miraculous to me. I'd never seen people like that before. Sometimes I studied them like an actor would, noting their postures, their sneering or sleeping faces, but I wasn't very gifted. I was observant, but I couldn't act. When the bus reached the beach, I'd get off and run up and down the stairs that led from the street to the shoreline. I'd take off my shirt, lie out on the sand, catch some rays, look at the water for a minute, then take the bus back home.

In the evenings, I bussed tables in a pizza parlor on Beverly Boulevard. Nobody important ever came in. Mostly I brought out baskets of bread and carafes of box wine, picked up pizza crusts and grease-soaked napkins. I never ate the food there. Somehow that felt beneath me. If I didn't have to work and there was a game going on, I'd take the bus out to Dodger Stadium and walk around just to get a feel for the crowd, the excitement. Nearby, in Elysian Park, I found a spot on a little cliff where I could listen to the cheers from the crowd and watch the traffic on the freeway, the mountains, the pale gray and sandy terrain. With all those ugly little streets in the ravine down below, LA looked like anywhere. It made me miss Gunnison. Sometimes I'd smoke a joint and walk around the swaying eucalyptus, peek into the cars parked along the fire road. Sedate, unblinking Mexicans sat in jalopies in shadows under the trees. Middle-aged men in dark glasses flicked their cigarettes out their windows as I passed. I had some idea of what they were doing there. I did not return anyone's leers. I stayed out of the woods. At home, alone, I concentrated on whatever was on television. I had a black-and-white mini Toshiba. It was the first big thing I'd ever bought with my own money back in Gunnison and the most expensive thing I owned.

My landlady's name was Mrs Honigbaum. When I lived with her, she would have been in her late sixties. She wore a short dark blond wig and large gold-framed eyeglasses. Her fingernails were long and fake and painted pink. Her posture was stooped in the shiny quilted housecoat she wore when she walked around. Usually she sat behind her desk in a sleeveless blouse, her thin, spotted arms swaying as she gestured and pulled Kools from a tooled leather cigarette case. Her ears and nose were humongous, and the skin on her face was stretched up toward her temples in a way that made her look stunned all the time. Her makeup was like stage makeup, or what they put on dead bodies in open caskets. It was applied heavy-handedly, in broad strokes of blue and pink and bronze. Still, I didn't think she was unattractive. I had never met a Jew before, or anyone intellectual at all back in Gunnison.

Mrs Honigbaum rented rooms in her house for forty-five dollars a week to young men who came to her through a disreputable talent agent – my agent. Forty-five dollars a week wasn't cheap at the time, but my agent had made the arrangements and I didn't question him. His name was Bob Sears. I never met him face-to-face. I'd found him by calling the operator back in Gunnison and asking to speak to a Los Angeles talent scout. Bob Sears took me on as a client 'sight unseen' because, he said, I sounded good-looking and American over the phone. He said that once I had a few odd gigs under my belt, I could start doing ad work on game shows, then commercials, then bit roles on soaps, then small parts in sitcoms, then prime-time dramas. Soon Scorsese would come knocking, he said. I didn't know who Scorsese was, but I believed him.

Once I got to town, I called Bob Sears nearly every weekday morning to find out where to go for auditions and what time to be there. Mrs Honigbaum let me use the phone in her bedroom. I think I was the only tenant to have that privilege. Her bedroom was dark and humid, with tinted glass doors looking out onto the swimming pool. Mirrors lined one wall. Everything smelled of vanilla and mouthwash and mothballs. A dresser was topped with a hundred glass vials of perfumes and potions and serums I guessed were meant to keep her youthful. There was a zebra-skin rug, a shiny floral bedspread. The ceiling lamp was a yellow crystal chandelier. When the door to the bathroom was open, I saw the flesh-colored marble, a vanity covered in makeup and brushes and pencils, a bare styrofoam head. The light bulbs were fixed along the edges of the mirror, like in backstage dressing rooms. I was very impressed by that. I went in there and studied my face in that lighting, but only for a minute at a time. I didn't want to get caught. While I was on the phone with Bob Sears, the maid sometimes flitted in and out, depositing stacks of clean towels, collecting the crumpled, lipstick-smeared tissues from the waste bin by the bed. The phone was an old rotary, the numbers faded and greasy, and the receiver smelled like halitosis. The smell didn't really bother me. In fact, I liked everything about Mrs Honigbaum. She was kind. She was generous. She flattered and cajoled me, the way grandmothers do.

B ob Sears had said I'd need a headshot, so before I'd left Gunnison, my mother drove me to the mall in Ephraim to have my portrait taken. I had a lazy, wandering eye, and so I wasn't allowed to drive. She drove me resentfully, sighing and tapping her finger on the steering wheel at red lights, complaining about how late it was, how hard she'd worked all day, how the mall gave her a headache. 'I guess in Hollywood they have chauffeurs to drive you around and servants to make your food,' she said. 'And butlers to pick up your dirty underwear. Is that what you expect? Your Highness?'

'I'm going to Hollywood to work,' I reminded her. 'As an actor. It's a job. People really do it.'

'I don't see why you can't be an actor here, where everybody already knows you. Everybody loves you here. What's so terrible about that?'

'Because nobody here knows anything,' I explained. 'So what they think doesn't matter.'

'Keep biting the hand and it might slap you across the face one day,' she said. 'Boys like you are a dime a dozen out there. You think those Hollywood people will be lining up just to tie your shoes? You think you're so lucky? You want an easy life? You want to roller-skate on the beach? Even the hairs on your head are numbered. Don't forget that.'

I really did want an easy life. I looked out the window at the short little houses, the flat open plains, the sky purple and orange, blinding sparks of honey-colored light shooting over the western mountains where the sun went down. 'Nothing ever happens here,' I said.

'You call fireworks over the reservoir nothing? How about that public library you've never once set foot in? How about all those teachers who I had to beg not to fail you? You think you're smarter than all them? Smarter than teachers?'

'No,' I answered. I knew I wasn't smart back then. Being an actor seemed like an appropriate career for someone like me.

'You're running out on your sister, on Larry,' said my mother. 'What can I say? Just don't get yourself murdered. Or do. It's your life.' She turned up the radio. I kept quiet for the rest of the drive.

My life in Gunnison really wasn't that bad. I was popular and I had fun, and pretty girls followed me around. I'd been like a celebrity in my high school – prom king, class president. I was voted 'most likely to succeed' even though my grades were awful. I could have stayed in Gunnison, gotten a job at the prison, worked up the ranks, married any girl I chose, but that wasn't the kind of life I wanted. I wanted to be a star. The closest movie theater was in Provo, an hour and a half away. I'd seen *Rocky* and *Star Wars* there. Whatever else I'd watched came through one of the three TV channels we had in Gunnison. I didn't particularly like movies. It seemed like hard work to act in something that went on for so long. I thought I could move to Hollywood and get a role on a show like *Eight Is Enough* as the cool older brother. And later I could be like Starsky in *Starsky and Hutch*.

I explained all this to the photographer at the mall. 'People say I look like Pierce Brosnan,' I told him. He said he agreed, handed me a flimsy plastic comb, told me to sit down and wait my turn. I remember the little kids and babies in fancy clothes in the waiting room, crying and nagging their mothers. I combed my hair and practiced making faces in the mirror on the wall. My mother went to Rydell's and came back with a new rhinestone belt on. 'Discount,' she said. I suspect she lifted it. She did that when she was in a bad mood. Then she sat down next to me and read *People* magazine and smoked. 'Don't smile too much,' she said when it was my turn with the photographer. 'You don't want to look desperate.'

Oh, my mother. A week later she drove me to the bus stop. It was barely five in the morning and she still wore her burgundy satin negligee and curlers in her hair, a denim jacket thrown over her sunburnt shoulders. She drove slowly on the empty roads, coasted through the blinking red lights as though they didn't exist, stayed silent as the moon. Finally she pulled over and lit a cigarette. I watched a tear coast down her cheek. She didn't look at me. I opened the car door. 'Call me,' is all she said. I said I would. I watched as she pulled a U-turn and drove away.

Gunnison was mostly empty fields, long gray roads. At night the prison lights oriented you to the north, dark sleeping wolves of mountains to the east and west. The south was a mystery to me. The farthest I'd ever gone down Highway 89 was to the airport, and that was just to see an air show once when I was a kid. I had never even left Utah before I moved to Los Angeles. I fell asleep on the bus, my little Toshiba under my feet, and woke up in Cedar City when a fat man got on and took the seat next to me. He edged me against the window and chain-smoked for three and a half hours, his body roiling and thundering each time he coughed. In the dim bus, flashes of light bounced off the mirrored lenses of his sunglasses, smudged by fingers greasy from the doughnuts he was eating. I watched him pick out the little crumbs from the folds of his crotch and lick his hands. 'The Garden of Eden,' he said. 'Have you been to Vegas?' I shook my head no. All the money I had in the world was folded up in the front pocket of my jeans. The bulge there embarrassed me. 'I go for poker,' the man gasped.

'I'm going to Hollywood to be an actor,' I told him. 'On television, or in movies.'

'Thatta boy,' he replied. 'The slimmest odds reap the highest payouts. But it takes balls. That's why I can't play roulette. No balls.' He coughed and coughed.

This cheered me to hear. I was bold. I was courageous. I was exceptional. I had big dreams. And why shouldn't I? My mother had no idea what real ambition was. Her father was a janitor. Her father's father had been a farmer. Her mother's father had been a pastor at the prison. I would be the first in a succession of losers to make something of myself. One day I'd be escorted through the streets in a motorcade, and the entire world would know my name. I'd send checks home. I'd send autographed posters from movies I starred in. I'd give my mom a fur coat and diamonds for Christmas. Then she'd be sorry she ever doubted me. We crossed into Nevada, the blank desert like a spot on a map that had been rubbed away with an eraser. I stared out the window, imagining, praying. The fat man caressed my thigh several times, perhaps by accident. He got off in Las Vegas, at last, and a black lady got on and took his seat. She batted the smoky air with a white-gloved hand. 'Never again,' she said, and pulled out a paperback Bible.

I put on my earphones and busied my mind with the usual request: 'Dear God, please make me rich and famous. Amen.'

Mrs Honigbaum was a writer. Her gossip column, 'Reach for the Stars', ran in a weekly coupon circular distributed for free in strip malls and car washes and laundromats around town. The gossip she reported was unoriginal – who got engaged, who had a baby, who committed suicide, who got canned. She also wrote the circular's monthly horoscopes. She said it was easy to steal predictions from old newspapers and switch the words around. It was all nonsense, she told me.

'You want voodoo? Here.' She pulled her change purse from a drawer and fished out a penny. 'The first cent you've earned as an actor. I'm paying you. Take it, and give me a smile.' Once she even made me sign one of my headshots, promising that she wouldn't sell it, even when it was worth millions. 'Don't get too attached to who you are,' she said. 'They'll make you change your name, of course. Nobody's name is real out here. My real name was Yetta,' she said, yelling over the clamor of her TVs. 'Nobody here calls me that. Yetta Honigbaum, can you imagine? First I was Yetta Goslinski. Mr Honigbaum –' She pointed to a small golden urn on top of her filing cabinet. 'Now I have no family to speak of. Most of them were gassed by the Nazis. You've heard of Hitler? He had the brains but not the brawn, as they say. That's what made him crazy. I was lucky. I escaped to Hollywood, like you. Welcome, welcome. I learned English in six days just reading magazines and listening to the radio. That's brains. And believe it or not, I was a very pretty girl once. You can call me Honey. It's a lonely life.'

She said she didn't believe in fate or magic. There was hard work and there was luck. 'Luck and hard work. Good looks and intelligence. In this city, it's rarely a two-for-one.' I remember her telling me that the day I moved in. 'Any fool can see you're handsome. But are you smart at all? Are you at least reasonable? That counts for a lot here. You'll catch on. Did you see this?' She held up the cover of a flimsy magazine showing Jack Nicholson picking his nose. 'This is good. This is interesting. People like to see celebrities at their worst. It brings the stars back to earth, where they belong. Listen to me. Don't go crazy. I should warn you that there are cults in this city, some better than others. People ask you to open a vein, you walk away. You hear me?' She made me fill out a form and sign my name on a letter stating that if anything happened to me, if tragedy struck, she would take no responsibility. 'I don't know what they teach you in Utah, but even Jesus would get greedy here. The Masons, the Satanists, the CIA, they're all the same. You can talk to me. I'm one of the good ones. And call your mother,' she said.

I had no desire to speak to my mother. I took a mint candy from the crystal bowl on Mrs Honigbaum's desk. 'My mother and I don't really get along,' I said.

Mrs Honigbaum put down her pen. Her shoulders slumped. I could see the fringe of her real hair poking out from under her wig in short gray tufts across her forehead. Tight bubbles of sweat, murky with makeup, studded the deep lines of her wrinkled cheeks. 'You think you're the first? My mother was a terror. She beat me black and blue, made me chew on bars of soap any time I mouthed off. She forced me to walk miles in the rain to get her plums from a tree, then beat me because they were full of worms. And yet I mourn her passing. I'm a grown woman, and still I cry. You only have one mother. Mine got starved to death and thrown in a trench full of rotting corpses. You are lucky yours is still living. If I were a Christian I would cross myself. Now go call her. You know she loves you.' And still I didn't call.

I felt safe at Mrs Honigbaum's house. I trusted her. She said there'd been an incident only once. A girl had stolen one of her rings. 'It was a ruby, my mother's birthstone,' she told me dolefully. Because of that, it was forbidden to bring guests into the house. I had a lock on my door but I never used it. There was a guest bathroom all the tenants shared. We had to sign our name to book shower time on a piece of paper taped up in the hallway. Mrs Honigbaum never gossiped about the tenants, but I had the sense that I was the one she liked best. One tenant was a voice actor for some cartoon show I'd never heard of. He walked around barefoot and shirtless, perpetually gargling and speaking in a falsetto, to keep his vocal chords from seizing, he explained. There was also a man in his thirties, which seemed ancient to me at the time. He was always widening his eyes as though he'd just seen something unbelievable. He had deep creases in his forehead as a result. I saw him carrying a painting to his car once. It was a portrait of Dracula. He said a friend was borrowing it for a music video. Another guy was an aspiring makeup artist. He always wore flip-flop sandals, and I could hear him flapping up and down the hall at odd hours. Once I caught him without any clothes on, thrusting his genitals into the cold steam of the refrigerator. When I cleared my throat, he just turned around and flapped back down the hall.

My room was next door to Mrs Honigbaum's office, so from morning to night I could hear celebrity news blaring from her six or seven televisions. The noise didn't really bother me. Every morning when I passed her open doorway on the way to the shower, her maid would be spraying the carpet where the poodle had shat. Stacks of old tabloids flapped in the breeze from an industrial-sized fan. The poodle was old and its hair was yellowed and reddish in spots that made it look like it was bleeding. It was always having 'bathroom mishaps', as Mrs Honigbaum called them. Whenever Rosa the maid saw me without a shirt on, she covered her eyes with her hands. Mrs Honigbaum sat at her desk and stared at her television screens, sweating and taking notes. It seemed like she never went to bed.

'Good morning,' I'd say.

'A sight to behold,' exclaimed Mrs Honigbaum. 'Rosa, isn't he beautiful?' Rosa didn't seem to speak English. 'Ah! My menopause,' Mrs Honigbaum cried, shoveling barium supplements past her dentures. 'Thanks for reminding me. Look at you.' She shook her head. 'People will think I'm running a brothel. Go get yourself some lemonade. I insist. Rosa. Lemonade. Donde está la lemonade?' With all the rejection I got at auditions, it was nice to be home and be somebody's favorite.

One afternoon, as I was coming in from tanning, Mrs Honigbaum invited me to dine with her. It was only five o'clock. 'Someone was going to come, so Rosa cooked. But now he's not coming. Please join me, or else it will go to waste.' I had the night off from work, so I happily accepted her invitation. The kitchen was all dark wood, with orange counters and a refrigerator the size of a Buick. The white tablecloth was stained with coffee rings. 'Sit,' said Mrs Honigbaum as she pulled the meat loaf from the oven. Her oven mitts were like boxing gloves over her tiny, knobby hands. 'Tell me everything,' she said. 'Did you have any auditions today? Any breaks?'

I'd spent most of the day on a bus out to Manhattan Beach where Bob Sears said a guy would be expecting me at his apartment. I arrived late and rang the doorbell. When the door opened, a seven-foot-tall black man appeared. He plucked my headshot out of my hands, pulled me inside, took a Polaroid of me without my shirt on, gave me his card and a can of 7-Up and pushed me out the door. 'It was a quick meeting,' I told Mrs Honigbaum. 'I didn't have many lines to read.'

She slid a woven-straw place mat in front of me, plunked down a knife and fork. 'I'm glad it went so well. Others have a harder time of it. They take things too personally. That's why I know you're going to make it big. You've got a thick skin. Just don't make the same mistake I made,' she said. 'Don't fall in love. Love will ruin you. It turns off the light in your eyes. See?' Her eyes were small, blurry, and buried under wrinkled, blue-shadowed lids and furry fake lashes. 'Dead,' she affirmed. She pointed upward to the ceiling. 'Every day I mourn.' She cleared her throat. 'Now here, eat this.' She returned to the table with a dinner plate piled high with meat loaf. I hadn't eaten a home-cooked meal since Gunnison, so I devoured it quickly. She herself ate a small bowl of cottage cheese. 'That is kasha,' she said, pointing to a boiling pot on the stove. 'I would offer you some, but you'll hate it. It tastes like cats. I make it at night and eat it for breakfast, cold, with milk. I'm an old lady. I don't need much. But you, you eat as much as you can stomach. And tell me more. What did Bob say? He must be very proud of you for all you're doing. I hope you're going to call your mother.'

I still hadn't called my mother. By then I'd been in Los Angeles for several months.

'My mother doesn't want to talk. She doesn't want me to be an actor. She thinks it's a waste of time.'

Mrs Honigbaum put down her spoon. Under the harsh light from the hanging lamp over the kitchen table, her fake eyelashes cast spidery shadows on her taut rouged cheeks. She shook her head. 'Your mother loves you,' she said. 'How could she not? Just look at you!' she cried, raising her arms. 'You're like a young Greek god!'

'She'd be happier if I came home. But even if I did, she wouldn't love me. She can't stand me most of the time. Everything I do makes her angry. I don't think she'd even care if I died. There's nothing I can do about it.'

'It's impossible,' cried Mrs Honigbaum. Her rings clanked as she clasped her hands together as if in prayer. 'Every mother loves her son. She doesn't tell you she loves you?'

'Never,' I lied. 'Not once.'

'She must be sick,' said Mrs Honigbaum. 'My mother nearly killed me twice, and still, she loved me. I know she did. "Yetta, forgive me. I love you. But you make me mad." That's all. Is your mother a drinker? Does she have something wrong with her like that?'

'I don't know,' I answered. 'She just hates me. She kicked me out,' I lied some more. 'That's why I came here. I just figure acting is a good way to make a living, since I can't go home. And my dad's dead.' That was true.

Mrs Honigbaum sighed and adjusted her wig, which had fallen off-center with all her gesticulating. 'I know what it means to be an orphan,' she said gravely. Then she stood up from her chair and came to me, the sleeves of her housecoat skimming the table, knocking over the salt and pepper shakers shaped like dancing elves. 'You poor boy. You must be so scared.' She cradled my head in her thin arms, squishing the side of my face against her low-slung breasts. 'I'm going to make some calls. We're going to get you on your way. You're too handsome, you're too talented, too wonderful to be squandering your time working at that pizza place.' She leaned down and kissed my forehead. Then I cried a little, and she handed me a chalky old tissue from her housecoat pocket. I dried my tears. 'You'll be all right,' said Mrs Honigbaum, patting my head. She went and sat down and finished her cottage cheese. I couldn't look her in the eye for the rest of the night.

The next day I picked up a copy of the coupon circular where Mrs Honigbaum's columns were published. I found one at the pawnshop across from the bakery where I bought my cinnamon doughnuts. Then I boarded an express bus going east on Melrose. I took a window seat and lay the circular across my lap. Mrs Honigbaum's columns ran side by side on the last page. I found my horoscope. 'Virgo: You will have trouble with love this week. Beware of coworkers talking about you behind your back. They could influence your boss. But don't worry! Good things are in store.' It was nonsense, but I considered it all very carefully. The gossip column was just a list of celebrity birthdays and recent Hollywood news items. I didn't know anybody's name, so none of it seemed to be of any consequence. Still, I read each and every word. Suzanne Somers is suing ABC. Princess Diana has good taste in hats. *Superman II* is out in theaters. As I watched the people of Los Angeles get on and off the bus, I felt for the first time that I was somebody, I was important. Mrs Honigbaum, who cared so much about me, wrote columns in this circular that traveled all across the city. Hundreds if not thousands must have read her column every week. She was famous. She had influence. There was her name right there: 'Miss Honey'.

Oh, Mrs Honigbaum. After our fourth dinner together, I found myself missing her as I lay on my bed, digesting the mound of schnitzel and boxed mashed potatoes and Jell-O she'd prepared herself. She made me feel very special. I wasn't attracted to her the way I'd been to the girls back in Gunnison, of course. At eighteen, what excited me most was a particular six-inch length of leg above a girl's knee. I was especially inclined to study girls in skirts or shorts when they were seated beside me on the bus with their legs crossed. The outer length of the thigh, where the muscles separated, and the inside, where the fat spread, were like two sides of a coin I wanted to flip. If I could have done anything, I would have watched a woman cross and uncross her legs all day. But I'd never seen Mrs Honigbaum's legs. She sat behind her desk most of the time, and when she walked around, her thin legs were covered in billowy pants in brightly colored prints of tropical flowers or fruit.

One morning, I stopped off at Mrs Honigbaum's office on the way to the shower as usual.

'Darling,' she now called me, 'I have something for you. An audition. It's for a commercial or something, but it's a good one. It could put you on the map quick. Go wash up. Here, take this.' She came out from behind her desk and handed me the address. Her handwriting was large and looping, beautiful and strong. 'Tell them Honey sent you. It's just a test.'

'A screen test?' I asked. I'd never been in front of a real movie camera before.

'Consider it practice,' she said. She looked me up and down. 'What I wouldn't give,' she said. 'That reminds me.' She went back to her desk and rifled through her drawers for her pills. 'To be young again! Well, go shower. Don't be late. Go and come back and tell me all about it.'

It took me several hours to get to the studio in Burbank. The audition was held in a small room behind a lot that seemed to be a place where food deliveries were made. The whole place smelled faintly of garbage. Two slender blond girls sat in folding chairs in the corner of the room, both reading issues of *Rolling Stone*. They wore tight jeans and bikini tops, huge platform sandals. The director was middle-aged and tan, his chest covered in black curls, eyes hidden behind dark sunglasses. His beard was long and unruly. He sat with a script open in front of him on the table, and barely lifted his gaze when I walked in. 'Honey sent me,' I said. He didn't stand or shake my hand. He just took my headshot and flicked his cigarette butt at the floor.

He must be doing Mrs Honigbaum a favor by allowing me to audition, I thought. He could have been a former tenant of hers. If he'd be reporting back to her, I wanted to perform better than ever. I had to be perfect. I slowed my breathing down. I focused my eyes on the blue lettering on the cameraman's T-shirt. GRAND LODGE. The cameraman had huge shoulders and hair that flopped to one side. He winked at me. I smiled. I chewed my gum. I tried to catch the eyes of the girls, but they simply sighed, hunched over their magazines.

It turned out to be the longest and most challenging audition I'd ever had. First the director had the cameraman film me while I stood in front of a white wall and gave my name, my age and height and weight. I was supposed to say my hometown and list my hobbies. Instead of Gunnison, I said, 'Salt Lake City.' I had no real hobbies, so I just said, 'Sports.'

'What do you play – tennis? Basketball? What?'

'Yeah,' I said. 'I play everything.'

'Lacrosse?' the director asked.

'Well, no, not lacrosse.'

'Let's see you do some push-ups,' he said impatiently. I did ten. The director seemed impressed. He lit another cigarette. Then he told me to mime knocking on a door and waiting for someone to answer it. I did that. 'Be a dog,' he said. 'Can you be a dog?' I sniffed the air. 'What does a dog sound like?' I howled. 'Not bad. More wolf than dog, but can you dance?' he asked. I did a few rounds of the Electric Slide. The girls watched me. 'Needs work,' the director said. 'Now laugh.' I looked around for something funny. 'Go. Laugh,' he said, snapping his fingers.

'Ha ha!'

He made a mark on the paper in front of him. 'Now be sexy,' he said. 'Like you're trying to seduce me. Come on, like I'm Farrah Fawcett. Or some chick, whoever, some girl you want to lay. Go.' He snapped his fingers again.

I'd never had to do anything like that before. I shrugged and put my hands in my pockets, turned to the side, pursed my lips, winked at him. He made another note.

'Come in for a close-up,' the director said to the cameraman. 'Stand straight, dammit,' he told me. 'Don't move.' The camera came about six inches from my face. The director stood up and came toward me, squinted. 'You always got zits up there between your eyebrows?'

'Only sometimes,' I answered. I tried to look at him, but the lights were too bright. It felt like I was like staring into an eclipse.

'Your eye's messed up, you know that?' he asked.

'Yeah, it's a lazy eye.'

'Work on that,' he said. 'There's exercises for that.' He sat back down. 'Now be sad,' he said.

I thought of the time I saw a dead cat on the street in Gunnison.

'Be angry.'

I thought of the time I slammed my thumb in the car door.

'Be happy.'

I smiled.

'Be brave. Be goofy. Be stuck-up.' I tried my best. He told me to stick out my tongue. He told me to close my eyes, then open them. Then he told me to kiss the two girls. 'Pretend they're twins,' he said. He clapped his hands.

The girls stood up and came toward me.

'You. Stand on the line,' the director said to me. 'That line.' He pointed to a length of black tape on the concrete floor. The girls stood on two Xs marked in red tape in front of me. They looked young, maybe sixteen, and pretty in a way girls hadn't been back in Gunnison. The skin on their faces was orange and as smooth as plastic. Their eyes were huge, blue, with wide black pupils, white liner drawn across their lids like frost. Their heads were big and round, necks and shoulders narrow and bony. I chewed my gum and put my hands in my pockets.

'What are you chewing?' one of the girls asked.

'It's gum,' I said.

'Get in the shot,' said the director. 'On the line. Jesus.'

'That's rude,' the other girl said to me.

'Take out the gum!' the director yelled. 'Let's do this. We haven't got all day.'

I took out my gum and held it on the tip of my finger and looked around for a place to throw it out. The girls sighed and rolled their eyes. The camera came closer.

'Action!' the director cried.

The girls lifted their chins.

I just stood there holding my gum, looking down at the legs of the table where the director was sitting. I was paralyzed. The girls laughed. The director groaned.

'Just kiss,' he said.

I couldn't do it.

'What, you don't like blondes? You've got a thing?'

I waved my finger around helplessly. I suddenly felt I couldn't breathe.

'I'll count to ten,' said the director. 'One, two, three . . .' I looked into the lens of the camera and saw my upside-down reflection. It was like I was trapped in there in the darkness, suspended from the ceiling, unable to move. I looked at the girls again. Their lips were frosted in pale pink, mealy and shimmering, nothing I'd ever want to kiss. Then one of the girls bent down to my finger and sucked my chewed-up wad of gum into her mouth. I took a step back. I was shocked. I tripped on a cord. The girls tittered. 'Ten!' the director shouted.

I did not get the part.

On the way home, I boarded two wrong buses, going east all the way down through Glendale and Chinatown. I walked through downtown Los Angeles, past all the bums and garbage, then finally found a bus on Beverly back to Hancock Park. At home, I walked straight into Mrs Honigbaum's office. I could have been irate that she'd sent me there. I could have blamed her for my humiliation. But that didn't occur to me. I just wanted to be soothed.

'It was bogus,' I told her. 'The director was some hippie. There wasn't even a trash can to throw my gum out in.'

'You win some, you lose some,' is all Mrs Honigbaum said.

'I'm a good kisser too,' I told her. 'Do you think Bob Sears will be mad?'

'Bob Sears doesn't know his face from his armpit. Let me see your mouth.' She got up from her desk and pointed to a chair. 'Sit. I promise I just want to take a look. Now open up.' I did as I was told. I closed my eyes as she peered inside. I could smell her breath, acrid from cigarettes and those harsh mints I'd grown fond of. She hooked a finger into my gums, pulled my bottom lip down, her long nail tapping against my two front teeth. 'All right,' she said finally. I opened my eyes. 'You have nothing to worry about.' She removed her finger, turned and went and sat back down at her desk. I took a mint. 'I'll tell you a secret,' she said, sharpening her pencil. 'Teeth are what make a star. Teeth and gums. That's the first thing they look at. That director is a fool. Forget about him. You?' She shook her head. 'You're too good for that guy. Good gums. Good mouth. The lips, everything. My teeth are fake, but I know a thing or two, and you've got the proportions.' She turned back to her pad of paper, flicked a page of a magazine, lit a cigarette. I stood. It was a relief to hear I wasn't doomed for failure, but I was still all torn up inside. If I failed to make it as an actor, where would I go? What else could I do with my life? Mrs Honigbaum looked up at me as though she'd forgotten I was still sitting there. 'Are you going to cry, darling?' she asked. 'Are you still upset about the kissing?'

'No,' I answered. I wanted her to embrace me, hold me tight. I wanted her to rock me in her arms as I wept. 'I'm not upset.'

'Is that what you wore to the audition?'

I was in my usual getup: leather loafers, tight jeans, and a loose Indian shirt that I thought made me look very open-minded.

'Stuff the crotch next time,' she said. 'You'll feel silly but you won't regret it. Half of a man's power to seduce is in the bulge of his loins.'

'Where's the other half?' I asked. I was completely sincere. By then I'd kissed half a dozen girls in closets at parties back in Gunnison but had never gone all the way. I never had enough enthusiasm to do all the coaxing and convincing it seemed necessary to do. And I was too anxious, too attached to my dreams of stardom to get tangled up in anybody's private parts. Of course, I thought about sex often. I kept a condom in my wallet, like an ID card. My stepfather had given it to me on my last night in Gunnison. 'Don't go and pierce your ears or anything,' he'd said, and punched me in the arm.

'Power is in the mind,' Mrs Honigbaum was saying, patting her head, jangling her bracelets. 'Read an hour a day and you'll be smarter than me before you turn twenty. I used to be too smart, and it made me miserable. So now I spend my time on soft stuff, like gossip.' She held up a copy of the coupon circular. 'It's all fluff, but I'm good at what I do. So-and-so is retiring, this one has cancer, that one is going crazy. *The Love Boat*, can you believe it?'

'Believe what?'

'It's nothing. Go have a cry, then come back and I'll tell you a story.'

'But I'm not going to cry,' I insisted. I flashed her a big smile to prove it.

'You go. Have a cry. If you want to talk after, come back. Have another mint.'

I retreated to my room to smoke a joint out the window and listen to the Eagles for a few hours. And I did cry, but I never told Mrs Honigbaum. In the evening, I went to work and tried to get those blond girls out of my head. Women left lipstick smears on their pizza crusts and the rims of their wine glasses, cigarette butts rattling in their cans of diet soda, phone numbers scribbled on cocktail napkins, smiley faces, Xs and Os. Their winks and tips did nothing for my low spirits, however. At home, I stared at my headshot and tried to pray for solace: 'God, make me feel good.' I cried some more.

In the morning I called Bob Sears. He mentioned nothing of my failure from the previous day. 'I received a call from your mother earlier this morning,' he said instead. He told me that she'd threatened to call the Los Angeles police. If I didn't call her that day, she'd open a missing persons case. 'She seemed very upset and inquired as to my qualifications as a talent agent. I told her, "Madam, I've been doing this work for forty-seven years and none of my boys has ever gone missing. Not under my watch." I'm not going to send you out into the lion's den now, am I? How could I profit? How?'

He gave me the addresses for two casting calls that day, neither of which I went to. I still didn't feel good. My head hurt. My face was swollen from crying. I spent the rest of the morning in front of the Toshiba, watching *Hollywood Squares*, *Family Feud*, all the while imagining my mother's rage. 'It was Larry's birthday last week. What, now you're too good to call? You think you're better than us, than me, your own mother?' I knew she'd be furious. I had nothing to say for myself. I had promised to call, and I hadn't called. Maybe I wanted to make her worry. Maybe I wanted her to suffer. 'I've been scared to death,' I imagined she'd say. 'How dare you do this to me. What have you been doing? Ballroom dancing? Champagne and caviar? Fooling around with who – whores?' I walked back and forth to the doughnut shop, feeling like a criminal. I didn't go out to the beach. I just crawled back home into bed, under the covers and listened through the blanket to *Days of Our Lives*, *Another World*, *Guiding Light*. Again I cried. At six o'clock, Mrs Honigbaum knocked on my door.

'I just got off the phone with Bob Sears,' she said. 'It's time to call your mother. See if she still hates you. Use the phone in the bedroom. Follow me.'

Mrs Honigbaum led me down the softly carpeted hallway and ushered me into her chambers, which I'd never seen at night before. The poodle scurried under the bed. Mrs Honigbaum turned on the chandelier, and suddenly everything was cast in dappled yellow light. The perfume bottles and crystal decorations glinted and winked. She slid open the heavy glass door to the backyard to let in some air. 'It gets stuffy,' she said. The room was filled with a fragrant breeze. It was nice in there. She pointed to the bed. 'Have a seat,' she said. Just then the phone rang.

'Who's calling me now?' she murmured. She plucked off one earring, handed it to me, and lifted the receiver. 'Hello?' I held the large golden earring in my open palm. In its center was an opalescent pearl the size of a quarter. 'All right. Thank you,' she said quickly, and hung up. 'It's my birthday,' she explained. She took the earring and clipped it back on. 'Now, sit here and call your mother. I'll be your witness. It'll be fine. Go ahead.'

She stood there watching me. I had no choice but to pick up the phone.

'Very good,' said Mrs Honigbaum after I'd slid the tip of my finger into the number on the rotary. 'Go ahead,' she said again.

I dialed.

The phone rang and rang. Nobody was answering. It was a Saturday night.

'See, no one's home,' I said to Mrs Honigbaum, holding the receiver out toward her.

'Leave a message,' she said. She lit a cigarette. I nodded and listened to the brassy bells dinging on the line, ready to hang up if my mother answered. Mrs Honigbaum exhaled two huge plumes of smoke through her flared nostrils. 'A good message.'

Finally the machine picked up. I heard my mother's voice for the first time in months. I held the phone out to Mrs Honigbaum again. 'That's her, that's what she sounds like,' I said. 'She always sounds so mad.'

'Never mind,' said Mrs Honigbaum.

After I heard the beep, I started my message: 'Hi, Mom, it's me.' I paused. I looked up at Mrs Honigbaum.

'I'm so sorry I haven't called,' she whispered. She waved her hand at me, smoke dotting the air, as though to spur me ahead.

'I'm so sorry I haven't called,' I repeated into the phone.

'My life out here is fabulous. I am making some major progress in my acting career.' Mrs Honigbaum widened her eyes, waiting for me to proceed.

I repeated what she said.

'And I'm meeting lots of fascinating characters.'

'I'm meeting fascinating characters.'

'I'm safe and eating well. There's nothing you need to worry about.'

I delivered these lines word for word.

'Please don't call Bob Sears again. It's not good for me, professionally.'

'Please don't call Bob Sears again. It's not good for me, professionally.'

'I love you, Mother,' said Mrs Honigbaum.

'I love you,' I said back to her.

'Now hang up.'

I did as I was told.

'There, that wasn't so hard now, was it?' Mrs Honigbaum extinguished her cigarette and sat down beside me on the edge of the bed.

'She's not going to like it,' I said.

'You've done your duty. She'll sleep better now.' My heart was racing. I bent over and put my head in my hands. 'Take some deep breaths,' Mrs Honigbaum said, a hand rubbing my back. I sat and breathed with her and I felt better. 'Now listen. I have something I've been meaning to show you,' she said. 'I don't show this to many people. But I think you deserve it. It's something to make you smarter.'

Then she reached across my lap and opened the drawer of her bedside table. She pulled out a sheaf of index cards. 'It's a special deck of cards I made myself,' she said. She shuffled through them. They were blank on one side, and on the other side they bore strange symbols – mostly shapes, solid or outlined or striped or polka-dotted, in different colors. Mrs Honigbaum had drawn them all in Magic Marker. One card had three green diamonds. Another had two empty red circles. A black solid square, a striped purple triangle, and so on. The point of the game was to set the cards down in rows and find patterns between the shapes and colors, what have you. 'This game is a metaphor for life,' Mrs Honigbaum explained. 'Most people are dumb and can't see the pattern unless it's obvious. But there is always a pattern, even when things don't make sense. If you build your brains up, the people here will think you're a genius. Nobody else is going to teach you how to do this. You'll see what I mean.'

She laid out three rows of three cards each on the bedspread.

'The pattern here is easy. Three of the cards have wiggly lines on them.'

I nodded.

She collected the cards, then laid out three more rows. 'This set is a little more mysterious. You see these three?' She pointed to three of the cards. One was an empty blue square. One was a solid red rectangle. The other was a striped green star. 'Sometimes the pattern is that they're all different. Do you see that? These three have nothing in common, and that's exactly what they have in common. Understand?'

I said I did.

'This is how to succeed as an actor. Point out the hidden pattern. Find meaning in the mess. People will kiss your feet.' I watched her pick up the cards again. I didn't understand what she meant at the time, but I could tell that what she was saying was true. 'Practice practice practice. You've got the brawn, now work on the brain. You want the big time, don't you? The big roles?'

'Yes,' I answered, though by then I really didn't. When she looked up at me, I stared deep into her small, blurry eyes. 'Thank you,' I said.

'No need to thank me,' she replied. She shuffled and laid down more cards, pointed to three circles. 'Easy,' she said, and clucked her tongue.

Then she was quiet. She shuffled the cards. She looked at me and shook her head. I thought maybe she was lost in her own reveries and would tell me a story about her dead husband or something funny that happened when she was young. But instead, she put down the cards, placed one hand on my knee, the other over her tanned, bony chestplate. 'Your mother is a lucky woman to have such a boy,' she said, exhaling as though it hurt her to admit such a painful truth. She lifted her hand from my knee and caressed my face, lovingly, reverently, and shook her head again.

Nothing ever happened under the covers of Mrs Honigbaum's bed, but from then on, each night before I fell asleep, she recited some prayers in Hebrew and put her hands on my face and shoulders. Whatever spells she cast, they didn't work. Neither of us was very surprised. ∎

© MOTOI YAMAMOTO
Labyrinth, 2012
Courtesy of the artist

KRAPP HOUR (ACT 2)

Anne Carson

Cast: various pairs chatting while they wait in audience for show to start

[1st]

if you're talking to Sylvester about African art don't call anything an *idol* it drives him nuts

Sylvester's descended from kings

so he says

walks like a king sits like a king

has king rages

what's he so angry at

his father

ah

whose advice was go to law school so he took up art

ANNE CARSON

painting sculpture what

connoisseurship

which means

art deals big money *the brand package* but also stupid museum labels
that *call everything an idol because they've no idea what it is*

hmm

I heard he ran away from home with his best friend at age seven

ran away where

and his dad brought them back

I bet

and next day arranged for the beheading of the best friend

no shit

and he made Sylvester watch

this was in Africa

it wasn't Winnipeg darling

you're gossip central aren't you

I was at one of those dinners Dave gets invited to

oh me too that's how I met Isabelle Huppert

no

I thought I told you this

so what's she like

she talked all the time about Jean-Paul Sartre

why

she met him

so what's he like

she said he talked all the time about John Huston

why

Huston invited Sartre to his house to work on some movie but Marilyn Monroe cancelled so they spent two weeks in Galway alone together in the rain

how'd that go

they fell immediately and deeply in love

you're kidding

yes I'm kidding Sartre called Huston a heap of ruins and Huston said Sartre had a face like an omelette

oh look there's Louise

where

ANNE CARSON

straight ahead of us about four rows

is that Louise oh you're right new haircut is she still seeing that kid

I think it's him next to her

I thought you were going to have a talk with her about that

chickened out

how much younger is he

last week he was writing her eulogy

what do you mean

she came into his room he was bent over the page really puzzling
what to put in what to leave out

all those loose bloody ends

I suppose

did you ask her what they talk about the two of them

no

did you ask her if waiters make a point of saying *hello madam how nice
you're out with your son today*

no

should do that

you're so judgemental

I'm just concerned for Louise

oh sure

you get that parchy tone

parchy isn't a word

yes it is

no it isn't

I met a parchy guy in Taos once his name was Larry Littlebird

great name

he had a bus tour business

you took a bus tour why

he looked nice I don't know he used to hang around the hotel lobby no one else took the tour we went to different pueblos mostly I remember him telling me *you live a room service life all white people are carrion*

I'm seeing why no one else took the tour

after that I felt odd paying for his orange juice

why were you paying for his orange juice

we were at the pool

what's this got to do with Louise

nothing I was just thinking about who looks down on who

whom

whom

so you fired Mr Bird

no actually after that he got to like me

part of his hustle

took me to his mother's pueblo we talked all afternoon I still think of
her sometimes it was a blazing silver afternoon

does Louise still have her dog

Philip Larkin yes

something wrong with calling a dog Philip Larkin

there's that tone again

[2nd]

she started doing the bones when

few years ago

where'd she get bones do you know

Dave told her where to get them

can I ask her about that do you think

be careful

or the bathtubs

be careful asking

Dave says he never met a more raw person

I saw her once on TV

the cracked teeth the dyed red hair the big black Reeboks

yes and they showed her studio

I'm supposed to go there tomorrow for the interview

just her in a big studio all these objects in rows and her on a stool in
the midst

doing what

working

shit

what

I'll be interrupting the work she'll hate me

are you scared

ANNE CARSON

I've no idea what to say to her

say *tell me about the vests Betty the bones the bathtubs*

tell me about your son dying ping ping ping is this an interview she'll
hate me

on TV her hands would go up and down when they asked questions

up and down

grappling sort of

she'll hate me

they just wasted away she said

who

I don't know she said it a couple of times *they just wasted away people
just wasted away*

might as well not even take my notebook

they asked about the bones and she laughs

laughs

oh the bones she says *oh the bones meant something to me* and she laughs
or more like caws as if

as if what

as if I don't know what

as if anybody knows how to talk about art

well there's that

I'll skip the bones

they say she's kind-hearted

that makes it worse you have to drink tea and split a kind heart apart at the same time

push push push I remember she said *push push push*

in reference to what

some question, her working method or *what's next for you now Betty* something like that

I won't ask questions

you could just sing

sing

she's a haunted person

why do you say that

from seeing her on TV maybe not haunted wrong word

what then

non-exempt

ANNE CARSON

non-exempt from what

life

the rest of us are exempt

yes

news to me

blind deaf dumb same thing

this is your theory of art

this is my theory of her awake all night worrying about little wild
animals active in the dark to which the rest of us are paying not very
much attention at all

I'll just have tea and leave

also you could ask Dave he used to know her

she was a patient of his once wasn't she

before my time it was Darly on the desk then

who's Darly

don't you remember Darly, Darly was a hoot she still calls Dave now
and then to give him the low-down on the man upstairs

upstairs where

Dave's other building she says about ten every night he's dragging a piece of heavy furniture across the floor

who Dave

not Dave the man upstairs then he drops pins or walks around in high
heels or has a lot of other people walk around in high heels tap tap tap
Darly's pretty sensitive to noise

got that

you ever meet him the man upstairs Dave says to Darly *no* says Darly
and Dave says *someday you'll meet him you'll say what was it with all
the pins he'll say those weren't pins and tell you some weird inside physics
fact you never heard of*

well you can't help but fantasize a man upstairs

[3rd]

where'd you get that shirt

Dave lent it to me for the dinner party

what dinner party

last week

lucky you it's vintage

he said *skip the lecture just go to the party half the people do that* he says

have any fun

ANNE CARSON

I end up talking to this Berlin journalist who translates crime fiction
on the side or did

nice life

until he couldn't find a non-obscene German equivalent for 'she
crossed her legs' and got fired

stop snapping that button

it was the dinner where I met the actress

what actress

Isabelle Huppert I thought I told you

you met Isabelle Huppert

sat across from her anyway

and

weird chick

why

lots of really white make-up like a doll and four red tears down one
cheek

stage make-up she must have come from the theatre

and she ate mostly salt

salt

this poor waiter serves her dinner gives it a big shake of salt starts to leave the table she waves him back he pours on more salt then I guess it's her husband takes the shaker pours salt all over finally she grabs it herself no let-up on eating fork in one hand salt in the other she finishes that plate without lifting her head

stress

her husband winks at me as if to say *what a treasure*

d'you wink back

I told him that proverb Han told me

who's Han

Ken's girlfriend

oh the Chinese one

you marry a chicken you follow a chicken she says

you said *follow a chicken* to Isabelle Huppert's husband

it's more nuanced in Chinese

I suppose

Dave always says why go to these parties if I don't like the people but it's not that I don't like the people

Dave's not into celebrities

true but he did get obsessed with that guy from his high school who wasn't even famous

just outed for doing a job no one else can imagine doing

oh boy

change of subject

what's it like do you think being salt and having Isabelle Huppert
come down on you with her big red lips

you're in a weird mood

did Dave tell you about when he went to that guy's house

you know I went with him

you're kidding

we were just driving around one night

and

was Dave's idea to knock on the guy's door it being Christmas Eve

what's Christmas Eve got to do with it

nothing really but Dave says *well I went to high school with him what the
heck* so we knock the guy comes to the door in a sweater and one look
at his face I'm thinking this is a bad idea Dave whispers *pretend we're
carollers* but neither of us can sing the guy offers us a twenty

you take it

we have no basket or anything so he puts it back in his pants not suspicious yet just kind of sunk in himself and all of a sudden he says *you got to be tougher you want money you don't want money say so* and his voice is a shock

why

maybe it was the Christmas thing, guy had this Christmas music on inside his voice made me want to cry I don't know

Dave does get you into things

and I said to him after we're in the car again I said *you're still curious aren't you*

and

and he admits he's interested to see how the guy did his tree

shit

but then just after Christmas he gets a call from the guy or could have been his manager

torturers don't have managers

no well who knows but they want to make a movie of his life a documentary these two women from LA

movie of Dave's life

no the torturer's

but he didn't recognize Dave at the door you said

not at the time

he took you for idiots panhandling

I guess it came to him later

so Dave's in the movie

no I doubt he'll do it

hmm

but I bet he's curious

Dave's always curious

concept is these two women from LA want Dave to be the interviewer
talk to the guy reminisce about high school see where it goes

Dave couldn't interview a block of cheese

my view exactly

but that's what we thought about Darly and then she joined the army

you mean we thought it a poor choice on her part

yes

but she turned out to be fully capable

and happy enough from what I hear still I can't imagine Dave in
a movie I can't imagine Dave as an interviewer

Dave says the guy's retired now

as if that makes sense as if you can retire from torture

it's very physical work Dave says

I can just hear him say that

in his next-slide-please voice

first thing you know he'll be bringing the guy to the clinic for treatment

don't even think it

[4th]

old words make me sad

like what

carhop

I've never said *carhop* in my life

what about *cardigan*

my aunt wore cardigans my aunt Nell and she was sad

well there you go

or not sad but kind of bluish kind of dusky she always showed up at

ANNE CARSON

our house at dusk with her mysterious blue luggage and sat beside
me on the couch

why

you mean why on the couch

yes

so she could teach me the sleeper hold

what's the sleeper hold

you can totally paralyze your enemy with the sleeper hold

show me

she also taught me the word *confidential*

wasn't that a magazine

when I see the word *confidential* even now a whole atmosphere like a
Humphrey Bogart movie comes out around it

just put your lips together and blow

then one day she wasn't there any more she didn't visit maybe she
died it got all hush hush you know how they whisper together in the
kitchen and stop when you come in

the family shadow

no one ever said

aunts have a longitude

yes

unlike uncles

uncles come in groups my uncles I remember always grouped around
the stove on winter nights passing the whiskey watching the fire

storytellers were they

actually no they were mostly silent big silent men side by side sort of
rustling not much talk

I wonder are we better off with all our talk

any stories they had were stories about snow

the snow was mythic in those days

and I remember that icy path from the kitchen to the outhouse, no
one on it snow on it mother-of-God spotless in the moonlight

show me the sleeper hold

I can't

ah

she never got around to it

ah

I didn't know how to ask for things

that's the whole trick isn't it

no one knew how to ask each other anything

families are a mystery

shot of whiskey for the boy not much else ever said

you often mention the outhouse why is that

no I don't

yes you do

some Freudian thing is what you're implying

not implying anything I merely wonder why you always mention the
outhouse was it a two-seater

ours was a two-seater yes

so you could sit and shit alongside somebody else

theoretically

did you do that

never if I could help it

you preferred to be alone

I went there to read

lots of reading material in the outhouse

usually newspapers but I took my book with me

I can just see you heading down the path with a volume of Proust under each arm

I hated it but those were happy days

golden age

it burned down the summer of the fires

you crazy fuck don't look so sad

she never got around to it why do you think that was

is it important

yes

so maybe that's what it was

what

and I wonder where she got blue luggage in those days

I'm going to ask Dave

about luggage

no the sleeper hold he's a medical man he may know it

I wouldn't be surprised, unrelated question do you keep a journal

yes why

just curious why do you

the light is so remarkable some days I have to put it away

put what away

stop it bothering me the light

what kind of light would that be

I can't say

is it only light does this

I screen out the rest

Dave says that guy from his high school kept a journal they're using
a few pages of it in the documentary

I don't want to know

Mr Matt Talbot liked to record materials and durations

I don't want to hear about it I don't want to know his name

Dave says

not interested

don't be a coward

language is a curse

didn't Beckett say that

okay yes I'm ridiculous

he has a recurring stage direction 'brief laugh' Beckett I mean

what about Mr Matt Talbot how funny is he

I was trained to do what I do in accordance with my training I'm quoting
Mr Matt Talbot

a tautology

an extinction

you see how language betrays us

is that Beckett again

oh piss off

parchy

what are you staring at now

the shadow of your hands on the table it looks like –

a coffin

no, celery

well there we are then

yes there we are ∎

THE ARCHIVE

A visual data study project
(based on a story by Sebastià Jovani)

TRANSLATED FROM THE SPANISH BY NICK CAISTOR

W hat follows is the result of a painstaking work of *interpretation and recoding* of a literary text, namely the short story 'The Archive', which author Sebastià Jovani was kind and unselfish enough to allow us to use for the purposes of the present analytic study.

The aim of this study is to offer and to *visualise* a means of understanding the essential aspects of a literary text, avoiding the possible confusions, or a proliferation of diverging interpretations, to which a conventional approach (whether a formalist or a subjective-hermeneutic one) could give rise, with the resultant added difficulty of accessing the fundamental nucleus of the text and its basic taxonomy.

From this starting point, the text was submitted to different externalised readings, which were in turn parameterised as a series of *categories* and *data sets*, previously established as fundamental to any textual-literary process of analysis. Namely: the author's aesthetic and contextual reference points (in the case of those whose traces could be detected in a more or less objective manner, without the need to incorporate further readings to disentangle such influences); the narrative structure (understood here as a temporal sequentiality and a typology of voices); the relations and characterisations of the protagonists of said story; and the evolution of the intensity of the storyline (incident-arcs surpassing the narrative-descriptive average of the events narrated).

The data thus collected was then adapted into a series of visual images and diagrams, accompanied by their corresponding labels. The results displayed on the adjacent pages therefore constitute a reading of 'The Archive', which also provides a translation of the story into strategic coordinates that combine data analysis with a graphic synthesis in tune with the requirements for interactivity with cultural objects and phenomena that our media environment increasingly demands. In addition, we hope to offer *the most objective possible portrait* of the creative process and indeed of the *figure of the author.*

We wish from the outset to express our thanks to Sebastià Jovani for his collaboration in the project, as well as to all those professionals from the data-analysis team who have taken part in this exercise.

1. Mapped Network of Literary and Contextual Reference Points

Science fiction

Thrillers

Peter Weiss

J.M.G. Le Clézio

Franz Kafka

Essays

Contextual elements

2. Temporal Sequentiality and Narrative Voices

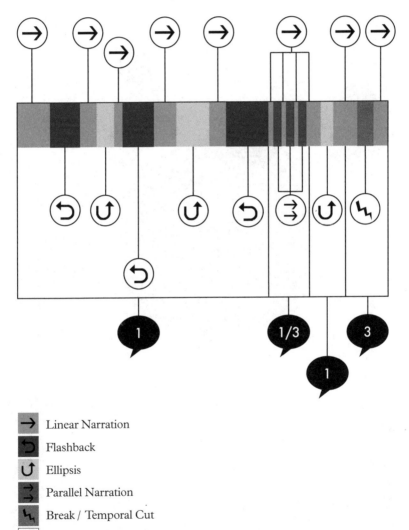

→ Linear Narration

↰ Flashback

↻ Ellipsis

⇉ Parallel Narration

↯ Break / Temporal Cut

🗨 Narrative Voice

3. Protagonists and their Characterisation

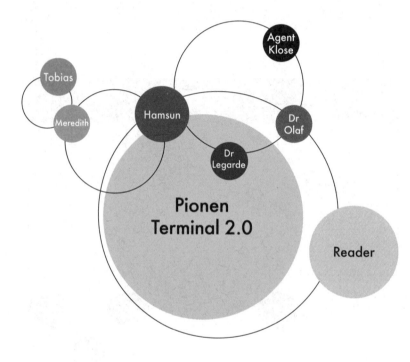

- Egotistic ➜ Expansive
- Anxious ➜ Angry
- Neutral
- Empathetic
- Candid
- Ambivalent
- Cunning
- Suspicious

4. Evolution of the Storyline and its Variable Intensities

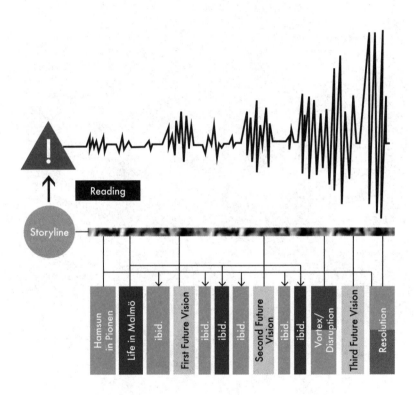

[Note: The chromatic choices for the distinct phases of the storyline correspond to those used for the analysis of sequentiality and narrative voices. This is to aid a better reading and localisation of data.] ∎

THE BUZZARD'S EGG

China Miéville

Good morning.

No? Are you still sulking?

Fine. Be sullen. It makes very little odds to me. I get my food either way.

Speaking of which. See how I light this? See how I put the right wood on it? How delicious is that smoke? I could turn my back and throw the embers over my shoulder at you and some people might say you deserve it, but I don't, do I?

You can see the day. I can feel your golden stare.

You don't intimidate me, looking at me like that. Keep looking over my shoulder too, through the windows. Don't you think our hills are beautiful?

I know they aren't your hills. But look how the sunlight hits the orchard. You can see the paths where Sirath's been walking. I think that's his name. I'm not sure. The man as old as me, with hair as grey as my eyes. There aren't many people around us here. Sometimes I hear a shout though, and he looks up. I think it's *Sirath* people call.

Go ahead, eat. I won't look. But do you see the rocks? By the overhang? Those gouges?

Priests and priestesses and soldiers and slaves came from the city – I told you, it's on the other side of the tower – a few months ago. They came with picks and took a whole slice out of the hill. The captain told me a new power was going to be born in the city, out of the mountain.

I don't remember his name. The captain's or the idol's, or if the idol was a he.

Those are eagles. And those, there? Buzzards.

A buzzard and an eagle loved each other. They hated each other but they loved each other too, and the eagle mounted the buzzard, and the buzzard laid an egg. And the buzzard didn't sit on the egg because she was proud. And a dove came and said, 'I'm such a fool, I must have lost this, my child.' She sat on the egg. 'How much bigger my children are than I remember!' she said. 'I can see the sea from up here.'

Have you eaten? Will you eat?

Please. Isn't the smoke delicious? You mustn't get sick.

The sea's forty miles east. I've never seen it. A trader came up the tower once – I don't know why the soldiers let him – and he told me what the sea was. His daughter was riding on his back. She was a tiny thing, and I stared at her until she cried, and he bent up and down and said to her that he was a boat.

So. The egg broke under the dove. What it was inside was a bird feathered with things like mountains and iron. It beat its wings and snow came down. It called and a rainbow came out of its mouth, I think.

Maybe you were there. Why won't you speak? Have I been disrespectful?

Will you do anything? Everything's just sitting there outside. That's just the wind in the trees, in and out, up and down, that's nothing. Sirath won't pick his fruit today.

It's a long way down to the courtyard. Do you see the well? That fountain used to run. Water came out of the mouth of that animal. I could hear it, even up here. It was nice. But then one of the soldiers got drunk – oh, some years ago – and he knocked into it and it didn't look like anything had changed but he must have bent its innards, because it never worked again.

He wasn't punished. There was no whipping. Perhaps his comrades covered for him. For a while mosquitoes bred in the last of the water. Now it's just stones down there.

I don't mean 'just' stones, I beg your pardon. Stones must be yours, back in your home, I think?

You have nothing to say? I know those shifts are the light of the sun behind the clouds.

You're like a child. I don't care if you're finished or not. Look at your bitter face. I'm taking your smoke away. I have things to do. You aren't the only thing in my day.

Be alone then. Go on. Watch the day go, then.

D on't look at me like that, it's just a cloth. It's dusty up here when the winds come – are they visiting you? Did you call them?

Not my business. I just think your face should be clean.

My hand's steady even though you're my enemy. Most people are afraid to do this, you know. They wouldn't touch you.

It's nothing. Look at you: you should shine.

I'm sorry about this morning. I'm not saying you didn't provoke me but I shouldn't have shouted. That's all, we don't need to make a whole story of it.

You're hardly my first prisoner of your kind. The soldiers of our city – it takes a lot to stop them. Your little place didn't have a chance, and your people must know that.

Because – I mean no disrespect, but hear me out – your realm's small.

You're clean water, yes? Fresh water and full trees? Woods full of game? The streets of your city, yes?

There are five rooms in this old tower. Spiral stairs for the height of a tree, then the mess, then there's the armoury, then three rooms like this, one on top of the other, swaying in the wind as you go up. All with heavy wooden doors that shake the walls when you slam them.

This is the middle room. Both of the others are empty. The one below I sleep in. The one upstairs only has a bit of rubbish left in it.

There've been times when none of them have had prisoners in them, and times when all three have been full. You can see the niches in the walls. Years ago – before those soldiers down there were even born

– the city was rushing in all directions and eating up everything it came to, and taking hostages from everywhere. Our troops would sweep through a city, kill its defenders, take its tributes, lay down new laws and then, to make sure the citizens behaved, they'd take the likes of you.

So downstairs there might've been the she-god or he-god of a city known for its woodwork, or a god of all babies. There was a lizard-headed fury upstairs once, a god of war. No disrespect but he was better made than you. His wings were lapis and black on the gold. He had a mace in his right hand. He was crushing birds and bones with his left. Very fine, heavy work, lots of inlaid stones.

I looked after him too. Without favour or malice. I deserve to have that noted, that I do my job well. Don't I light your fires every morning and every evening?

Never mind what happened to him. His people – how could they fight when we had him? When their god of war was gone? So that city's ours now.

Can you feel your people? Can you feel them worshipping? Are they sad? Are they frantic? Are they afraid for you? Does the worship reach you?

Look, down goes the sun again – someone else has that in hand, you see. Don't tell any priests I said a word about any of this. Though no one should be angry with an old man for speculating. Down goes the sun again and it's all shadows left, like giant blocks.

How are you? Are you lonely? Or do you like to be alone?

You don't have to tell me anything.

The thing is – don't think me cruel, I'm just too old not to tell the truth – I look at you and I know what I see.

You aren't embarrassing. Your work isn't good, though, either.

Some of those we've had here, there's no way I could even carry alone, and I was strong once. They were as tall as I and the metal on them was thick, with too many gems to count.

Now I'm not going to say we've had none cruder than you. Our forces took a village – the people who lived there called it a city but I'm sorry – some huts in the marsh by the dead forest. And the soldiers brought back their god here, to keep them quiet.

I felt sorry for it. It was wood and clay about the size of my arm, and I could barely tell what it was, it was so worn. There may have been bronze on it once but that was gone. It looked at me with two little stub eyes of some green stone. I mean pebbles, polished pebbles. It could break your heart.

They loved it, their poor swamp god. They loved it and I can tell you, I could tell, I knew, that they didn't know what to do. Whether they should surrender and beg their little god back, or whether they should keep on warring for it – because they were still fighting us from the dead trees, even with it gone, they had camps in that forest of useless ghosts.

I fed it smoke as carefully as I do you. They surrendered, of course.

Our priests handed it back. They weren't disrespectful to it. Ugly thing. I hope it's ruling its soggy patch, bringing its people fish.

So I'm not going to tell you you're the weakest I've guarded. I've tapped you with my nails. There's thick enough metal over your wood, a decent mix of gold. Those agates in your face are small but well cut. That ivory's elegant.

But you're little, from a little place. I mean no disrespect. Are your people worshipping you? They can't free you. It must be you're supposed to do things like keep the canals clean. They must be very dirty now. I'm sorry. That worship must be snagging you.

I'm telling you this so that you can tell the people lamenting in your temple.

Send them dreams. Are those dreams you're sending them, over there, going westward, or are they bats? Tell your people to surrender, to behave, to give tribute. It won't be so bad. They can come and take you back.

I know you're kind. I'm grateful and you can't stop me being so. I've been here a long time and I see you. I'm sure you're austere and jealous too but I see you being kind to me. You don't have to say a word. You're a good god.

The soldiers talk to me sometimes, they aren't bad. Sometimes we sit up together and they ask me about who was here before, and tell me what's happening in the city. I cook their food and pour their wine, and sometimes they let me have a bit, diluted with milk or water.

I think if I left the tower and my feet touched the ground – which they know is forbidden – some of them would be unhappy to have to follow their instructions. I don't say they'd cry but I think they might say something like, 'Old slave! Why would you do that? Now look!' or, 'Old man! I regret this!' And then if they put piles of rocks over me after, or tipped me into a gully, they might say something rueful. Maybe they'd be upset, I don't know.

Maybe they'd say, 'Was he unhappy?' I talk about old sadnesses sometimes – no matter how often you say to yourself, 'No, this is yours, keep this yours, they needn't know, no one cares about your miseries,' it's hard to say nothing. So some of them might say, 'He had a child once and the child's gone.' They might say, 'He carried something with him, poor slave.'

They'll talk about how a man was taken when he was very young and had a tiny baby and a wife, when everything was starting. Taken from a place that called itself a city so it could have a god, and that its little god was taken with him, it as a hostage, he as a slave.

They'd have to report to the city that the jailer was dead – I don't like that word any more than you, but it's what they call me, when they don't call me slave. They'd have to wait here and perform my duties until a replacement was sent.

Oh, you should hope that doesn't happen! I can't help thinking of those rough young men polishing you, or burning your incense. Oh, woeful! I can't help laughing.

You don't need to look at me like that. I've no intention of walking out into the dirt, no matter that I'm tired.

You are kind. I see it in the cast of your eye. I see how wistful you are when you watch the sky. Is that a weapon you hold, or a crook to snag animals? Is it a pole to feel the depth of a stream?

There's lemon peel wrapped around the wood. It may spit, but I hope you like it.

Goodnight, god.

I could take weapons from the armoury, but what would I do? There's no getting past the soldiers. And they're my countrymen now, I suppose.

Officers come sometimes, from the city. And priests and oracles. Not very often, but when they have new hostages to jail, or sometimes to mark a ceremony or anniversary. They all sing, they go, *luh lah, cayya luh lah*, and so on. I could have learned the tune a long time ago, it's almost always the same song. I choose not to learn it. I'm not called on to sing. It amuses me to watch the soldiers rumbling away.

Once a high priestess and priest came and sang a different song. It was hot, for all the clouds and the storms. I was nearly as wet as they, even stuck under this roof, I was gushing with sweat as I followed them. They were old, older then than I am now, and he was bruised and had scabs on his arms and legs and she breathed hard, but they came quickly up the stone stairs to the captain.

They talked in the armoury. I brought them wine and moved slowly so I could listen. The holies were thoughtful and grim. The priestess kept her eyes on the storm.

'We'll get them,' she said.

'They took all of them?' the captain said. She said nothing so the priest hesitated and nodded.

'They fight well,' he said.

We were at war again. A small war against a fading port. Our battalions had stormed down the river and along the coast. But our enemies had sent their own men, in disguise, into our city. They killed the guards and godnapped our gods.

'Is that why all this shit?' the captain said, pointing out of the window at the hot rain. The old priest rubbed his eyes and hit the table with his fist. The priestess bared her teeth.

Was I alarmed? I don't think any more than a little. Our gods are well guarded, though, our soldiers well trained, our city fortified. I was surprised anyone had been able to take them.

Mostly I was curious. What would happen? All of them? The Queen of the Gods, the Great Farmer, the Clearer of Filth, the Soldier with the Whip, the Moon? They were *all* gone? That had to be bad. The Spirit of the City was gone? Without them, how could our soldiers fight? But they must fight, I thought. Would they be able to get our gods free? Would they negotiate? Pay ransom?

'Bastards,' the priestess said. 'Bastards and sons of bastards.' She sang a song I hadn't heard before and haven't heard since.

The rain didn't stop for twenty days. It ruined the crops. It sent a farmhouse sliding down the slope of the hill, taking the whole family with it but for a baby who was left squawling under a tree where her cot wedged.

I didn't see that: it was on the side where there are no windows. I heard the soldiers talking about it before they left for war. They checked their spears and their armour. They were relieved by a junior group who didn't know what they were doing and made a terrible mess. The wood they gathered was green and too young to burn.

Then the captain of the relief after *that* told me about working in the city's temple just before coming here, about how proud he'd been to serve in the presence of our gods. So I learned we had them back. I don't know what our city, where I've never been, did to retrieve them.

The old priest came back once. At the end of that year it was he who came to wish winter away and sing the usual song to the soldiers who stood shivering in the courtyard. I stood at the corner of the window in the lowest of the cells and watched them.

The priest was nodding as he sang. I remembered his anger. I remembered when his companion said, 'Bastards,' and I realised I didn't know if she meant the godnappers or the gods who'd let themselves be taken, who'd let everyone down.

Here: you have a smudge on your chin. There. And let me turn you so the sun isn't in your eyes.

I'm sorry I'm not very talkative. I dreamed of family, of quiet. It was a good dream.

Was that you?

If it had been up to me I'd have taken you to the uppermost cell. I could clear the rubbish out from the alcove – it wouldn't take long, I should have done it years ago – and put you there.

One of the soldiers here is very young and very boastful. I see him in the courtyard challenging all his comrades to wrestling matches. He's beaten at least one time in three and whenever he is he crows and complains and insists that there was cheating and that he won, really. He has no malice and they like him, and I do too. Sometimes I do little things for him. Anyway, he told me the war's over. This last war.

'There'll be people coming soon,' he said. 'We beat the other city and that's just that. Just as I was getting ready to fight, too.'

I'm telling you because I've seen the sadness in your gold eyes and I don't think you deserve it, though you're the god of my city's enemies.

So I want you to know that you'll be going home soon.

The war's over, and we won. There's no shame in it. The city always wins and almost always will. Your people are coming, so they must have paid ransom.

I hope they did.

It's nothing, you shouldn't worry at all. Don't pay me attention.

There was a time we destroyed the hostages.

Everyone agrees it was a terrible thing, so don't look like that, I beg you. No one would do it now. That war-god I told you about? He was broken apart.

It was a bad king who ordered that done, because he was angry with our enemies. Yes, it worked, it crushed them, but it was shameful.

I see you aren't afraid. You impress me.

I'm all right. You don't need to worry about me, not at all.

It's been good to know you. You've been an interesting guest. I know: prisoner. But let me consider you my guest? I'll be sorry when you go.

If I look a little sad, it's just that there are so many questions I should've asked, and I don't know how long we have now. I want to know about your family and your city. Your people, who worship you. Who are coming.

Why do you look sadder?

You'll be back with them soon. Don't you hear me?

You do. Shall I cover your eyes? Will you send bats to tell your worshippers where we are? Where you are, with me to talk to you?

This is the best wood I have. I've put all the perfume I have on it, and I've shaved it into little slivers as best I could with these old fingers. Aren't you enjoying it?

You know, it occurred to me – I have to say this quietly, and I shouldn't say it at all, which is why I have to whisper it into your metal ear – that maybe that soldier heard wrong. Maybe our city lost. Maybe your priests will come and kill the men downstairs and set you free and carry you back to your city on their shoulders in triumph.

I don't know if they'd consider me your enemy. Don't worry. I'm not worried.

But it doesn't seem likely. My city's armies are stronger, the gods are bigger and heavier and made of more gold.

And even if that is what's happened, that doesn't cheer you, does it?

God, why are you so sad? There was a little boy whose spirit ate the bones of his neighbours while he slept. Shall I tell you a story? Will you tell me stories? How do you rush across the valleys? When you fly, is it with the slow strokes of a heron? Do you scatter farms with blood? How do the hunters of your city honour you?

Oh you must remember the Washing of the Mouth! When one minute this was wood and gold, and then it was you. Do you remember, these eyes for you to see with, these hands, this staff you carry? When the people made you?

I'll tell you a story then. This is a story I tell myself from time to time. A tiny city was overrun by soldiers who took its little god and a very young local man to look after it. The two of them were locked away together. The man was sad because he'd seen the soldiers kill his family with swords and now he was without them. The god was sad for godly reasons. Because he'd let his people down and now their crops would rot, and because he knew how they'd come for him and look at him when they got him back and no one had ever asked him to god them.

The man cried and he was angry with the god. 'My baby's dead,' the man said. 'My wife is dead. What good are you? Set me free. You're the only god of my city so you're the god of everything. Harvests and war and childbirth and everything. And death. I'm too afraid,' the man shouted. There were knives in the armoury but he wouldn't pick them up. 'So you do it for me. Don't I worship you? Do it.'

The god felt the man's worship and, further away, the worship of his other people as they approached with ransom. It gave him no strength, it made him tired.

The man and the god watched from the top window of the tower. 'They're coming,' the man said, 'and you'll have to start doing your job again.'

The man looked into the god's silver eyes. The god looked into the man's grey. The man jerked like a toy, grabbed his chest, gasped and wheezed and fell down.

The priests and the soldiers of the victorious city came up the stairs, escorting the defeated holy men and women. They heard a great crash and a scream. They rushed into the top room.

Strewn across the floor were the remains of the captive god. The man had smashed it against the walls. It was all in pieces. Its wood was in splinters. Its metal was twisted. Its gems – and there were never many

– were scattered and broken. There in the middle of the rubbish stood the young prisoner. He was slapping the sides of his own body and his head, screaming and staring with wide eyes at his own hands.

The high priest assured his defeated enemies that this hadn't been his orders, that it was an insane action by this slave. Who was, he reminded them, one of their own countrymen. Nonetheless, the deicide brought a bit of shame to the priest. It had occurred under his city's authority. Of course their city had to stay under his city's control, but they could keep their ransom. And the slave, he told them, would be executed.

But when they'd gone, he looked thoughtfully at the young man, who was still gripping his own flesh as if it bewildered him.

'I'm going to have you whipped,' he said. 'But what happened? You hate gods now? All of them? Or just your own? For failing you?

'If you ever do anything like that again without instruction,' he said, 'I'll have you killed. But I need a slave who has a bit of scorn for gods. A bit of spite. Just enough not to be cowed by them.'

He had the young man whipped, and then he had him bandaged, and then he told him what his duties would be. And the new slave said to him, 'Not spite. Pity.'

D on't be afraid. Were you sleeping? I'm going to take my hand off your mouth now.

Can you see the moon?

Oh, thank you. You're kind. You are a kind god. Let me kiss your cold face.

Tonight I could hear the soldiers downstairs like snorting calves.

I heard them eating and laughing, shuffling in their blankets, and I started to hear them more and more clearly. I heard, I heard the secrets that floors and walls tell in their creaks. When I got up I don't remember, or how, perhaps I flew as if my feet had little wings, or as if my head was a cloud. But I was by the window and that moon talked back to me in its light.

There are things about the ways bodies see. There are things to be said for how flesh eyes see night and fail to see it. But to look through shadows to where the mountains are like the teeth of fishes again! Everything's silver like the metal that was upstairs on the floor a long time ago.

The soldiers are moving early. Visitors are coming with tribute for you.

Don't be sad, god. What you've done – it's such a thing. Follow my finger towards, yes, there, not a bat but a moth, and its heart rises in its little moth chest because it's in love. Geese will wake and cry in the day soon, and the lava in the ground will answer them.

I'll put my arms around you. These are old man's arms but let me carry you, my friend, let's rise, like when you fly. Yes you're heavy even though you're not so very gold but I don't care how heavy you are. I'm not as heavy as I was once either, or as strong, but I'll carry you.

Look. In the mountains are rock machines and rock ships with eyes, and we can see the edges in the seamless stone that separate those things from the rock that holds up the trees.

Your worshippers are coming. I know. Come up with me to the top room.

They're coming to buy your freedom, you small heavy god. Your city'll be a colony and your worshippers'll take you back.

Come in. That's only wood on the floor. All the scraps of silver they took away, years ago, to make more of their own gods in the city. That wood I leave there for nostalgia. To push it into my fingers.

You never heard my name and I never heard yours. It doesn't matter at all. Listen to what that angry cloud is telling you, the mutter of all the animals on the crest of the hill.

I can't remember: did a young man destroy his miserable god, or did a god free its worshipper and take his blood and his bones?

Well.

Let me put you here to talk to the sun, which is coming soon, to talk to it with your motionless golden mouth and the scatter of its heat on you. Let me put you down – these arms are shaking! – not in the alcove by the junk of an older god's body, but right here, out on the ledge as far as I can, so the wind worships you. That worship doesn't hurt? No. That you can bear a minute.

They'll call me mad again. Here come your worshipping people, and that's another thing: don't worry, you're ready, and no one will do anything for you or to you, you do it all, you're a god, you move in your ways. I'll put you one tiny bit closer to the air so the birds are ready for you.

And don't think me rude as I leave a little grease kiss on the back of your head and turn my back. This is your communion. I'm going to jump and dance – these old legs! The floor's vibrating, more and more now as here come the soldiers and your worshippers. Don't be sad, you needn't see: you are facing the other way.

My dance makes the tower shake. You quiver on your threshold.

They call out to you! How sad they are to see you move!

And you aren't sad any more. Thank you, you kind god.

So. Feathers like mountains, or knives, unfolded gold? Rush. ∎

Model Reconstruction of Ancient Rome

In the lower right is the Pantheon. We use a program called
    MODFLOW to model groundwater and pull down
of the aquifer. There isn't going
                to be much more water. The sun moves across the oculus
    as children dig holes in the garden.
Here I am. My name is Sadie. I am a 'mom'
    living in the 21st century. Mostly, I am not a poet
but today I have stolen a few hours from work.
  The structure of the whole
                is a symbol of the world.
    Arches spring up. Do you want to go to Sephora
    and get some fake eyelashes?
Here I am. Sephora, symbol of stolen work.

NOTICEBOARD

CONTRIBUTORS

John Ashbery is the author of more than twenty volumes of poetry. His new collection, *Breezeway*, is published this spring. A two-volume set of his collected translations from the French (poetry and prose) was published in 2014.

Jesse Ball's work includes the novels *Silence Once Begun* and *The Curfew*. 'The Gentlest Village' is an extract from *A Cure for Suicide*, forthcoming from Pantheon Books in July 2015.

Nick Caistor has translated more than forty books from the Portuguese and Spanish from authors such as José Saramago, Roberto Arlt, Andrés Neuman, Juan Marsé and César Aira. He is the editor and translator of *The Faber Book of Contemporary Latin American Short Stories*.

Kevin Canty is the author of three story collections and four novels, including *Winslow in Love* and *Everything*. His short stories have appeared in the *New Yorker*, *Esquire*, *Tin House* and elsewhere.

Anne Carson is a Canadian poet, essayist, translator and professor of classics.

Jon Fosse is an internationally renowned Norwegian writer and playwright. In 2007, he was made a Knight in France's National Order of Merit.

Janine di Giovanni is the Middle East editor of *Newsweek*. A war and conflict reporter for twenty-five years, she is a member of the Council on Foreign Relations and was recently made an Ochberg Fellow at Columbia University for her work on trauma victims. She also advises the United Nations Refugee Agency and the Geneva Centre for Security Policy.

Peter Gizzi's most recent books include *In Defense of Nothing: Selected Poems 1987–2011* and *Threshold Songs*. He teaches at the University of Massachusetts, Amherst.

Charles Glass was ABC News's chief Middle East correspondent from 1983 to 1993 and is the author of four books on the region, including the forthcoming *Syria Burning*.

Noémie Goudal's solo show, *The Geometrical Determination of the Sunrise*, will be presented at the New Art Gallery Walsall and at Foam Fotografiemuseum in Amsterdam.

Sebastià Jovani is a novelist, essayist and poet whose most recent book is the novel *Transnistria*. 'The Archive' was first published in Spanish in the latest issue of *Granta en español*, *Rebaño + 1 (Herd + 1)*.

Kathryn Maris's most recent poetry collection, *God Loves You*, was published in 2013.

China Miéville is the author of *The City & The City, Embassytown* and *London's Overthrow*, among many other works of fiction and non-fiction. His forthcoming collection is *Three Moments of an Explosion: Stories*, published in 2015.

Ottessa Moshfegh is the author of *McGlue*, a novella. Her first novel, *Eileen*, will be published in the US this year and in the UK in 2016.

Tracy O'Neill is the author of *The Hopeful*, published in June 2015. Her work has appeared in *Grantland, Rolling Stone*, the *Atlantic* and *Bookforum*. In 2012, she was awarded the NYC Emerging Writers Fellowship by the Center for Fiction.

Damion Searls translates from the Norwegian, Dutch, German and French. His translations of Jon Fosse include *Melancholy* (with Grethe Kvernes), *Aliss at the Fire* and *Morning and Evening*, as well as the libretto for an opera of *Morning and Evening*, premiering at the Royal Opera House in 2015.

Raja Shehadeh is a lawyer and writer. His books include *Strangers in the House, Palestinian Walks: Notes on a Vanishing Landscape* and, most recently, *Language of War, Language of Peace: Palestine, Israel and the Search for Justice*. He lives in Ramallah.

Sandra Simonds is the author of four collections of poetry: *Ventura Highway in the Sunshine, The Sonnets, Mother Was a Tragic Girl* and *Warsaw Bikini*. She is a professor of English and humanities at Thomas University in Georgia.

Arch Tait was awarded the PEN Literature in Translation Prize in 2010 for his translation of Anna Politkovskaya's *Putin's Russia*. To date he has translated twenty-seven books from the Russian, most recently the memoirs of Akhmed Zakayev.

Ian Teh has published three monographs: *Undercurrents, Traces* and *Confluence*. His work is part of the permanent collection at the Los Angeles County Museum of Art, the Museum of Fine Arts, Houston, and the Hood Museum of Art. *Traces II* was supported by the 2011 Magnum Emergency Fund and the 2014 Abigail Cohen Fellowship in Documentary Photography.

Ludmila Ulitskaya studied biology at Moscow University and worked at the Institute of Genetics until she was fired for dissident activities. She later became a scriptwriter and repertory director of the Hebrew Theatre of Moscow. She is the author of thirteen works of fiction, three tales for children and six plays. In 2001 she won the Russian Booker Prize.